MW01610884

PRAISE FOR
THE SYSTEMATIC TRADER

Collin has been at the forefront of trading education, contributing various articles to many media channels, including *Shares Investment*. With his new book, Collin takes trading education to the next level. From the very personable introduction down to various chapters that share various trading strategies, Collin's new book is bound to keep you in its grip with its useful actionable content. Take heed though, this is not a book which you can just read and chuck aside. The book essentially brings you on Collin's journey through trading and guides you through your own. A very captivating and useful tool for traders who want to start with success.

- Simeon Ang
Editor, *Tradeable*
www.sharesinv.com

The Systematic Trader helps traders understand what is most important to make excellent trades and investments in markets. Learn how to focus on the things that professional traders and investors do so you can make yours the best.

- Mike Bellafiore
Author, *One Good Trade* and *The PlayBook*
Managing Partner, SMB Capital
www.smbcap.com

This is a fantastic book that will have a profound impact on your trading. Not only does Collin share his proprietary trading system, he also drills the importance of understanding the systems that you use. This is of paramount importance, as only with a thorough understanding of the system used will a trader be able to make the necessary adjustments to suit different market environments. A great resource and highly recommended.

- **Marc Liu**
  Partner, TradersGPS
  www.tradersGPS.com

As a new trader, knowing how to make consistent profit in the market is always the pain. Collin uncovers this mystery for traders. The book is about you and the market, and tells you how to set up your mind to become a successful trader. If you are serious about trading, then you must read this book.

- **Shanison Lin**
  Founder, InvestingNote
  www.InvestingNote.com

It has been a while since someone comes along with a special ability to pack such vast important trading topics into a manner simple and easy to understand. With this book, Collin has just raised the bar big time in the trading scene. This book is a must read for traders of all levels.

- **Kyaw Sonic**
  Founder, Sonic R. Trading System
  www.sonicrsystem.com

This book contains the two most important topics in trading—trading a plan and framing a winning mindset. Do yourself a favour by understanding these and you will avoid the money losing traps in trading.

- Ng Ee Hwa
Director, Chartnexus
www.chartnexus.com

One of the few local financial writers that I follow and read, Collin's life experiences allow him to give us valuable advice, especially in the local context where many other books are simply about foreign markets. A must read for Singaporeans.

- Akay Sin
Private Investor

THE SYSTEMATIC
TRADER

How I Turned A $250,000 Debt Into
Profits Through Stock Trading

BY COLLIN SEOW, CFTe
WITH CHIN YONG SAK

Candid Creation Publishing

First published May 2015

Candid Creation Publishing books are available through most major bookstores in Singapore. For bulk order of our books at special quantity discounts, please email us at enquiry@candidcreation.com.

THE SYSTEMATIC TRADER
How I Turned A $250,000 Debt Into Profits Through Stock Trading

Author:	Collin Seow
Co-author:	Chin Yong Sak
Publisher:	Phoon Kok Hwa
Copyeditor:	Melanie Chua
Layout:	Geelyn Lim
Cover design:	Elieth Sardinas
Published by:	Candid Creation Publishing LLP
	167 Jalan Bukit Merah
	#06-12 Connection One Tower 4
	Singapore 150167
Website:	www.candidcreation.com
Email:	enquiry@candidcreation.com
Facebook:	www.facebook.com/CandidCreationPublishing
ISBN:	978-981-09-3476-7

National Library Board, Singapore Cataloguing-in-Publication Data
Seow, Collin, author.
The systematic trader : how I turned a $250,000 debt into profits through stock trading / by Collin Seow, CFTe, with Chin Yong Sak. – Singapore : Candid Creation Publishing, 2015.
pages cm
ISBN : 978-981-09-3476-7 (paperback)
1. Stocks - Handbooks, manuals, etc. 2. Stockbrokers - Psychological aspects. I. Chin, Yong Sak, author. II. Title.
HG4661
332.6322 -- dc23   OCN900431554

CONTENTS

ACKNOWLEDGEMENTS

I would like to thank first my God, who prompted me to write and complete this book. I want to also thank my co-writer Yong Sak, who pushed me along whenever I got struck; Kok Hwa, my publisher who advised me to not put in even more ideas and to complete the book; Alicia Yeo, my assistant in Phillip Securities who stuck with me when everyone else had left; Marc Liu, the co-founder of TradersGPS; my mentor in trading (whose name I cannot reveal); my business partners, such as Chris Isaiah from Sharesinvestment, Shanison from InvestingNote, Kelly Clement, Dave Osmond, and Scott Brown from ChartNexus, Asa Soo, Steve Ng, Derick and Julia Liu from Phillip Securities; Henry Tan from Cyberquote; past SMT graduates such as Thomas, Justin, Xavi, and Mr Tan who helped me with the SMT community; the "My Money and You" Mastermind Group, Amos, Joe, Jonathan, and Jayson, who demanded more of me than I did myself; and my brothers and sisters in church, especially my leaders James and Lisa. Last but not least, my spouse who has patiently stuck with me through thick and thin.

FOREWORD

As a friend of Collin, I am very happy to see his first book published. Collin has been a great and passionate coach to many traders, holding countless workshops and seminars, and sharing his trading skills as well as views on the market.

I strongly believe his book contains the knowledge and valuable information many traders, new or experience, would need in order to excel in trading. I personally appreciate how he has delineated the "inner" and "outer" wars. This is what trading is about. But most traders focus only on the outer aspect, which is one of the key reasons why they keep going in circles. Be sure to finish the book and you will have a wider perspective on what trading means.

Another of his concepts I wish to reiterate is, do not blindly apply a system or trading black box. Understand each and every indicator or parameter used and why are you using them. Trading blindly will get you nowhere! This is the precise reason why in this book, Collin has explained each and every trading system in painstaking detail.

Every trader should understand their own personality. Pay attention to his personality test in Chapter 9. Before you complete a race, you must first identify the start point. Hence, before you start trading, you must first know yourself.

I am sure this book is of great value to readers. I highly recommend taking this journey to discover yourself, and the wars you will be facing, if you are serious in being a sustainable and profitable trader.

Patrick Liew
Managing Partner
Global Enterprise Exchange

Patrick Liew, MBA, MSc, BSc, is currently the Managing Partner of Global Enterprise Exchange. He is also a founder of Success Resources, arguably Asia's largest seminar organiser and a major shareholder of the company, which is listed on the Australian Stock Exchange. Through his team at Success Resources, Patrick has organised educational conferences for prominent leaders such as President Bill Clinton, Prime Minister Tony Blair, Michael Porter, Richard Branson, Robert Kiyosaki, Donald Trump, and many other prominent leaders.

Patrick provides leadership and advisory services to many professional and charity organisations. He is actively involved in supporting humanitarian, philanthropic, and charity causes. He has helped to organise many social missions and in the process, helped to set four records in the Singapore Book of Records and a record in the Guinness World Record.

PREFACE

When I finally paid off the debt of SGD$250,000, I thought to myself, "Wow! This story can be written into a book to inspire others who can't seem to see the light at the end of the tunnel." That was where my journey of writing a book started. But I had other priorities at that time. I almost forgot about it until Yong Sak approached me for an interview for his own book, *Secrets to Highly Profitable Traders*. I did not have any expectations for the book but it took off like a rocket. It became a National Top 10 bestseller. This was not for one week but for 24 consecutive weeks! In fact, it was the number one bestseller in Singapore for a couple of weeks. This really got me motivated to write my own book. Writing a book is not exactly the way to make money in Singapore. Compared to the effort put in, the reward is not great; the market in Singapore is too small. Nevertheless, I wanted to write this book because I wanted to share my experiences gained during my journey.

The book took too long. It was probably more than three years to finally get this book published. One problem was me constantly adding new ideas and experience learnt from the market. After I attended a course, "So You Want to be an Author", conducted by Kok Hwa, my publisher, I learnt that I could always keep the ideas for a second book.

Surely others will benefit from the skills and knowledge that I have learnt during this painful journey from failure to success. They say that a wise person learns by the experience of others, an ordinary person learns by his or her own experience, but a fool learns by nobody's experience.

It is my sincere hope that this book can benefit you in your journey towards success in trading and investing. This book contains the essence of what I know about trading and investing from almost 20 years in the industry. You will learn almost everything I cover in my courses: Systematic Trader course (SMT) and Phillip Trading Bootcamp (PTB), both organised by Cyberquote (the training arm of Phillip Securities Pte Ltd).

First, I share my personal journey on my thoughts about trading and what I have learnt. I think faith is important as we journey through the valley of darkness. Whatever that was emptied from you, you must believe it will be made full again.

In Chapter 3, I talk about the best instruments for protecting, saving, investing, and trading. You will learn a concept called "buy term and invest the difference" that I personally practise. Many of these concepts are financial planners' trade secrets. After years as a financial planner, I think this is one of my best takeaways from the industry. Being a remisier and professional trader, this book will focus on trading as well as investing.

In Chapter 4, I share a strategy learnt while still studying for my Certified Financial Technician (CFTe). One very successful hedge manager also showed me how to trade short term. In CFTe, we learn many different indicators but the essence can be found in two indicators. In fact, I strongly believe that these are the only two indicators you ever need to know to read a chart successfully.

I share my mechanical trading system in Chapter 4, an area I specialised in technical analysis. This system was previously available only for my SMT students. However, I have worked with TradersGPS to make the system available to the public. So now you can get this system without attending my course.

In Chapter 5, I share short-term trading strategies from Toby Crabel's book *Day Trading with Short Term Price Patterns and Opening Range Breakout*. You can find used copies on eBay for US$275; but if you want it new, it will cost you US$811. This is a powerful short-term trading strategy. Crabel Capital Management has over $1 billion in assets under management. Crabel is a professional trader and not a professional author or trainer.

In part two of this book I share how psychology is one of the important elements of trading. What are the practical things you can do to improve your trading psychology? One of them is being a good steward of money, which I learnt from the founder of Phillip Securities. It is not enough to knowing what to trade and how to trade, you also must know how much to trade or invest.

I developed a concept of the personality of traders about a year ago. I noticed, from my clients, that different people approach the market in vastly different ways. Knowing yourself is as important as knowing the market you are trading in. You will also learn how to create a winning community to support you.

Finally, at the end of the book, I share all my resources gathered over the years. This is not a complete list, but one that I believe will give you a headstart in your journey in trading.

Writing this book has been challenging for me because I am not a professional author. Thus, I want to thank all for your generous time and effort to make this book possible.

1 IT'S NOT JUST ABOUT MAKING MONEY

E ven when I was serving in the army, I had already started my career as a financial adviser. I got to know my manager, who shared with me about the "MDRT".

The Million Dollar Round Table (MDRT) is a global independent association founded in 1927. It has more than 42,000 of the world's leading life insurance and financial services professionals from over 470 companies and 71 countries. It is a very prestigious title and I wanted to have it. In fact, if I were to achieve that, I would be one of the youngest in the world to attain that title.

While most of friends were happy with a job, I wanted something more. My dad was old and I wanted to earn money fast to let him retire soon. I knew if I achieved the MDRT, my earnings could easily be double of what my peers were making.

Another reason to qualify for MDRT was the Annual Meeting held in different parts of the USA. I would represent Singapore to attend a worldwide meeting in Atlanta, USA. The MDRT Annual Meeting has been described as a one-of-a-kind event, unrivalled in the world of business. Every year, approximately 6,000 of the world's top producers gather in a spirit of camaraderie for one of the greatest gatherings of financial services professionals in the world. The desire to achieve my goal was so strong that I told my manager I would die if I did not qualify for the MDRT.

During that period, money was my key motivation and I was driven purely by material wants. Of course that made my manager extremely delighted as he was able to make much from my commissions. I got a portable bed to sleep on and spent nights in the office. I worked more than 100 hours a week. There was a contest to win a mobile phone— and mind you, during the era of pagers, having a mobile phone was a symbol of success!

While others were busy dating their girlfriends on weekends, I was meeting prospects to talk business. Believe me, I was doing whatever was needed to achieve MDRT. I spent the daytime meeting prospects and nights finishing up paperwork and setting up appointments for the following week. Almost every night, I took the last bus back home with a lethargic body. There were times when I missed the last bus, so the portable bed came in handy.

It was not an easy task as my peers actually had very little money for insurance or savings. I did not give up and forked over the hard work. My efforts paid off. I managed to qualify for the MDRT title! Indeed, I was one of the youngest in the world ever to be awarded it. Throughout the year, I had visualised my success and being there physically. When I was actually there in the hotel room, I could not fall asleep because it felt like I was living my dream, something I had been working so hard for and been thinking of every second.

The Reality

Even after winning that title, I continued to work and party hard. I partied until 4 a.m. and still arrived at the office early in the morning to call my prospects. Although my goals and targets were set higher each year, I was not saving enough. I was spending money faster than I could earn them. As a result, I had to work harder in order to keep up with my spending. It was such an irony that I was failing to be a good financial advisor to myself!

Despite the success, I was in a dilemma. The policies that paid the best commission were usually not the best for my clients. On one hand, I needed the commission to pay for my rising bills. On the other, I could not bear to sell my clients something I did not believe in.

One night after a late drinking session, I felt a heavy emptiness and loss. I felt like the proverbial rat on the wheel, chasing after money only to find that I needed to work even harder the next year just to keep up. I had an epiphany; I did not want to live my life like that anymore. I began writing about what I wanted to do and achieve with the rest of my life.

I wanted to be true to myself and find peace every time I go to sleep at night. I wanted to live a life I would be proud of when I leave this beautiful world. That night, I listed my action items as below:

1. Reduce my expenses.
2. Live a simple life.
3. Make money work for me.
4. Rest well.

A New Chapter of My Life

To achieve my new goals, I decided to invest in stocks. Warren Buffet was the person I would model myself after. Without any doubt, he is the best in the field of value investing. I bought and read every book about Warren Buffet and began applying all the new theories picked up.

I thought it would be just that simple, but I was wrong. One of the first stocks I chose was Informatics, one of the top private educational companies with a strong brand at that time. The financial numbers were very good. Many analysts gave a target price of $1.30 and I thought it would be a no brainer to buy it at $1.15. Guess what? Informatics is now trading at 0.096, far less than the price I bought. I was really fortunate that I cut loss when the price was around $1.00. Of course, I had other bad experiences in value investing. I started to doubt myself. I was unsure what I was doing wrong and began to feel lost.

Eventually, I pulled myself together and went back to the drawing board. While reflecting, I realised I learnt technical analysis much earlier, but had never thought of putting it to good use. I first learnt it from a commodity trading house, even before joining the Army. I started acquiring more knowledge on technical analysis and began seeing good results.

Being ambitious, I started to trade everything, from coffee to stocks to indices. I finally settled down and focused my efforts on trading indices and selected Singapore stocks. With some level of success, I decided to trade full time with the aim to live a simple and happy life. At the rate I was trading, I thought it would be a brilliant idea to be a remisier, so as to lower my own trading commission. On top of that, I could potentially gain more insights on the market. I was wrong!

While I was a remisier, I spent much time and effort on trading my own account and did not have many clients with me. I saw that it was too much hassle to "entertain" clients, jeopardising my own trading time. As I mentioned, I simply wanted to live a simple and happy life trading full time.

Maybe God Had Other Plans

About six months into the business, one of my clients was trading heavily in warrants where each position could be up to about $100,000. This client of mine was very good in his studies and entered the top school in Singapore. He wrote a worldwide paper sponsored by Lehman Brothers and won an award for it.

Good things do not last. He over traded and started to lose money, lots of money! Instead of cutting loss like a professional, he averaged down his price (like how most would), trying to win back what he lost. The long and short of it, the loss was unbearable. He finally closed his position, making a loss of about $250,000 in total.

The loss must have been so great for him that he decided to default that payment and was even ready to file for bankruptcy. He was confident that he would be discharged after a few years of bankruptcy. In this business, if the client does not pay, the remisier will have to. He encouraged me to file for bankruptcy with him, but I was not going to let this pin me down!

I had no one to turn to except God. My wife was then pregnant with my second child and I could not bear to tell her the situation. With my commission of just about $2,000 per month and interest of 9%, it would take me almost forever to pay off the debt. I resorted to renting out the master bedroom just to make ends meet.

During that down period, I read *Anointed for Business*, a book by Ed Silvoso. In short, this book was about putting Jesus first in life. Sometimes when things became unbearable, I would close the door, kneel by the chair and seek directions from God. I would pray in tears, asking God to give me the strength to carry on. But not only did God give me the strength I needed, he also gave me the grace to forgive.

That client decided to tour Australia for the last time before declaring bankruptcy. Instead of being upset with him, I met him at the airport to bid him goodbye. I told him that things happened for a reason and this incident would bring out the best in me. I did not have an answer yet, but was willing to follow God's direction. He was a very logical, academic person, and told me that God was a "man-created" idea.

During these trying times, I often went to the beach to reflect, do some thinking and plan for the next steps. I decided to stop trading discretionarily and to systemise my trades. I was going to find a trading method that would allow me to trade on a longer time frame. I also devised a plan to pay off my debts. The three key things that I needed to do were:

1. Do technical analysis training.
2. Acquire new clients.
3. Devise a systematic way of trading.

At this point, there is one interesting incident that I wish to share with you. While in a lift, I saw a family approaching and held the door for them. When the doors opened at their floor, I again held it to allow the family to exit. As the door was closing, one of the family members turned around and asked if I was a remisier! Not only that, he mentioned that he would be ready to open an account with me if I was one! I was caught by surprise with two questions in my head. *How did he know I was a remisier? Why would he want to open an account with me?* He did not become my big client but he referred another to me, who eventually became one of my biggest clients. At that time I was wearing three hats. I was a remisier, trainer, and investor rolled into one. Through hard work and God's grace, I was awarded the Top 10 in Phillip CFD. I am currently in my ninth year as a remisier and am in the Top 10 every year that the award has been given out.

Since I used technical analysis for my trades, I could impart the skills to others too. Without much experience in speaking or teaching, the first few trainings were really disastrous. During the trainings, I focused on more technical stuff such as trend lines, support and resistance, candlestick patterns, different indicators, etc. Some of my students were not making money despite applying exactly what I was teaching. I saw that the students were not cutting loss fast enough and not riding their profits long enough. It was then that I realised teaching the correct trading psychology was more important than just technical knowledge.

2 SECRETS TO SUCCESSFUL TRADING

My remisier business grew over time and was gathering more and more clients to me. As I grew my remisier business, I was also taking my Certified Financial Technician (CFTe) course. One of my classmates suggested doing a group study together. He was a very successful hedge fund manager. In fact, he was the owner of the fund. One day, when I visited him, he was in such a happy mood because he had just received $250,000 from Indofood IPO.

In one of the group study sessions, I happened to share my story with him. Perhaps out of sympathy, he pointed me to some valuable resources on trading and shared his experiences with me. With a humble learning attitude, I picked up much knowledge on trading from him.

It was him who made me understand that there is no such thing as a perfect system in this world. The only way to be, and to continue to be successful in trading is to add positions when winning and cut loss fast when losing.

In trading, there are only two important elements, the **Payoff Ratio** and **Probability of Win**. These are the only two things we traders can control. We have to leave every other condition to the market.

More on Payoff Ratio and Probability will be covered in later chapters.

With the plans I had laid out and through sheer hard work, I managed to pay off my debts in about 16 months. I was extremely delighted that this heavy burden was off my shoulders at last! I was very eager to share this piece of good news with that client (who had put me in debt), and was disappointed to be unable to contact him.

One morning while looking through my phone's stored data, I noticed that it was his birthday and decided to try my luck again. To my surprise, the line went through and he picked up my call. I excitedly told him that I managed to pay for his contra loss, but he sounded indifferent to it.

It was my faith and belief that pulled me through this crisis. Without the ability to forgive, I could still have been stuck in that nasty situation or, worse, declared a bankrupt. This, I believe, is my journey. If not for it, I might still be so fixated on myself and my own well-being, and that could have rendered me "useless" to society. It was through this crisis that I understood I do not live only for myself. The good news was that he was finally discharged, and on 2 January 2014, we met up for lunch. I am glad that throughout the whole episode, I had kept my faith and testimony to him.

Importance of Values, Knowledge, and Skills

I want to take this chance to share with you an important asset which I call **values**. A value is an asset or element that can determine if you attain sustainable success in trading. Therefore, it is essential that every trader work on their own values. Without the correct values, you will still fail regardless of how formidable your strategy is!

I noticed traders who trade well are those who are able to detach themselves from the results. This greatly reduces emotions from their trades. For me, I had already gone through rough times and was in terrible shape. Money became easier for me to manage because it was not so "important" anymore. This crisis caused a change in my values, helping to transform me into a successful and profitable trader today.

I cannot stress any more how important it is to possess the correct set of values for trading. If you think trading can make you super rich overnight with little effort, or that you can beat the market heads down every time, you will find yourself driving across the rough terrain of trading.

One of the values that I think helped me in trading and life is: **Don't focus on the money when trading.**

Even though trading deals with money, I feel that those who are concerned about making or losing money, lose it. You should focus only on being a good trader. When it is time to buy, you buy. When it is time to cut loss, just cut loss and do it quick! When it is time to take profit, take it, and do not be greedy hoping for more.

MONEY IS AN EFFECT, NOT A CAUSE

Next, **focus on being rather than getting**.

As you trade, focus on being a good trader rather than getting the profits. Once you are a good trader, money is a given, a by-product. However, if you are only concerned about making money, you will never be a good trader.

Failure is the mother of success

I think it was Thomas Watson of IBM, the American technology giant, who said, "To increase your success rate, double your failure rate." If you want to trade, the fact is that you will be wrong probably 20% to 50% of the time. If you don't want to be wrong, you will end up holding stocks that you should have cut loss much earlier, in turn causing you to lose more money. If you had followed your trading rules and the trade still went against you, pat yourself on your shoulder for a job well done and move on.

Trading is not about lifestyle

I see some traders advertising their trading courses, enticing others with their luxurious lifestyle. Real trading is not like that. Real trading is almost boring like any other job. It is quite boring in fact. People like to buy into dreams. For me, I don't see the need to do so, because what I want is to build a community of traders for the long term with the right knowledge, skills, and values, and help them work towards financial freedom. The key is the long term. Over time, they will know what is real and what is not. That does not mean the trading is not financially rewarding, what I am saying is that it should not be the focus when you are trading.

Trading is like a sport

The correct mindset in trading is to treat it like a sport. When a champion tennis player serves for the final match, he will not be thinking if he wins this point, what will be the reward he is going to get. The right mindset is to fight for every point and being present. This is the same as trading, when you are trading, you want make sure that you are doing the right thing at any point of time and not be swayed by emotions.

Ability to hold two or more conflicting thoughts at the same time

Trading is not black and white, rather more like shades of grey. You must think in term of probabilities. The challenge is that sometimes you need to execute a trade without full knowledge. You will need to make an educated guess (still following closely to your trading rules and money management) and let the market decide whether you are right or wrong.

Do the hardest thing first, or do the easiest thing first

If you can tackle the hardest thing, it will give you the momentum you need to finish the rest of the work. If you think that you cannot overcome the hardest thing, tackle the easiest thing, it will also give you the momentum you need to finish the hard work later.

Trading is not the end all

You need to have a life aside from trading. Again, it is like in sports or games. If you get too much into it, it starts to control you and wear you out. You need to know that at the end of the day, it is simply a game. Once you have this mindset, you are much stronger mentally.

Every "failure" is a chance to learn

Every time you cut loss, do not lose the opportunity to learn more about the market and yourself. Ask yourself: 1. *What happened?* 2. *What did I do right?* 3. *What can I do differently?* You can write this down for every trade you do, otherwise known as **trading journals**. By doing this, you can improve in your game much faster.

The problem is most are too concerned with how much money they will make or lose and cannot be bothered about the lesson to be learnt. In fact, I learn more from a losing trade than a winning trade. A fish cannot see the water that it swims in. A trader cannot see himself when he is trading. That's why it is important to review your trades.

Success is a habit

We are creatures of habits. If you want to be successful, build good habits. List down all the good habits that a good trader should have and ensure you practise all of these habits daily.

Have a routine

Every successful sportsperson has a routine. With a routine, you psych yourself and make sure you are ready for the next trade. I see this very often when tennis players get ready to serve a ball. You should also have a routine that you go through when you trade.

Face your fear and it will flee from you

Fear is only fearsome if you do not deal with it. Only when you face it and take action will it diminish. Actions replace fear. Your fear is nothing but imagination. Another way is to imagine the worst-case scenario, then face it. If you can handle that, anything less is a bonus.

Think often

The biggest problem now is that we do not think enough. I guess we are simply too busy sometimes to think. I have a routine to have my quiet time to think and reflect. Some like to keep a journal about what happened; others like to meditate. The idea is to think about what works for you. From Socrates: "The unexamined life is not worth living."

All these values that I share do not only apply to trading, you can apply them in life.

There is no "model" set of values for trading, as different traders will have different sets of values, depending on their lifestyle, needs, wants, etc. What are your values for trading? Are you able to list them when you are in a calm state of mind? After listing and reviewing them, would you be able to discuss with your mentor or peers?

Training helps me to consolidate and reinforce what I learnt and understood. As a trader, we should aim to simplify and compartmentalise what we knew or learnt. Every indicator says different things, tells different stories and because of that, many traders got confused. When you train others in trading, the knowledge and information you acquired tend to get "internalised".

To be successful in trading, you must also have **knowledge**—on the market, the instruments you are trading, the indicators you are using, and knowledge of yourself.

Through my experience in training, I reckon many traders are stuck at the knowledge level. They learnt a lot from various resources and attended countless courses and seminars. Needless to say, many ended up getting more confused from all the information gathered! The reason is because despite learning new things and acquiring new knowledge, they fail to transform it into **skill**.

Having "skill" is to apply what you have learnt, coupled with good understanding on how to filter what is necessary from what is not. It is also critical to know when and what to use or apply under different situations or conditions. If, for example, you are trading one-minute charts, using support and resistance lines might be more efficient than indicators like Stochastic Slow or RSI. It may not be a good idea to trade the trend as the period is simply too short to determine a trend.

It is very common for traders to have conflicting knowledge. This means they may learn a trend-trading strategy one moment and then a counter-trend strategy the next. Most traders will get confused by which strategy to use instead of looking into combining them seamlessly. To be able to apply multiple strategies, you need to have a good understanding of how each and every strategy works and under what market conditions they work! The other solution is to create or develop an automated programme to help one to make objective trading decisions.

Not surprisingly, I used to be a victim too, to be honest. I kept changing strategies every time when I learnt something new. I did not go through enough testing to verify if my current strategy worked before changing to another. Like many traders, I changed strategies because I thought that the new one was more powerful, giving me more winnings with no losses. All in all, I was guilty of constantly looking for the Holy Grail of strategy and indicator. Many traders fall into this trap. Are you one of them? If you are, what should you do now?

My turning point came about when I managed to determine what the fundamentals were in trading and what was "universally correct". What do I mean by this? Trend trading, in which my key intention is to follow or trade with the trend, in my opinion is universally correct.

The secret to successful trading is to decide quickly what you want or are comfortable with, settle down, and fine-tune what you have. Quit changing strategies as you will end up going in circles!

Most strategies work in the long run, as long as they have good Payoff Ratios and high Probability of Win. Give the strategy ample time to verify that they actually work. What many traders (who failed) do is to hop from one strategy to the other when they suffer one, or more, losing trade. The brutal fact is, there will always be losing trades, no matter how formidable your strategy is. **Accept this fact and you will gain sustainable success in trading; ignoring it will make you go around in circles and achieving nothing but losing money to the market.**

Stewardship or ownership

As traders, we must understand that there will be losing trades for every 10 trades made. The irony is most traders cannot accept this fact! They are not at all tolerant of losses, which keeps them searching for strategy after strategy. To be honest, it will be easier to trade if you can accept the fact that losses in trading are inevitable. Because of this known possibility, you are less likely to overtrade and will be in better control of your fear and greed.

On this topic, it brings me to discuss stewardship and ownership with you. Between fund managers and retail traders, who do you think will do better? All my bets go to the fund managers. This is because the fund manager's role is to keep his job by trading strictly by the rules of the trading firm. A fund manager, in this case, is a steward.

On the other hand, most retail traders feel that they are the bosses of their money. They want very much to control all decisions and, worst of all, outcomes. It will be hard for them to cut loss as it is a sign that they are wrong. They feel that losing their hard-earned money is out of the question. This makes following rules extremely challenging for them and breaking their own rules is the best choice.

When the market is bad, retail traders refrain from trading as they are fearful. They fear losing their money. On the other hand, fund managers continue trading according to rules, as that is their job. To be successful and profitable in trading, we must change our mindset and values. We are not the owner but stewards of money. How well you manage this money will greatly determine your trading results. Be a steward of money and focus on trading well instead of focusing on the dollars and cents. I reckon a change in values is like a paradigm shift. Traders who changed their values to the right direction are less likely to break their trading rules and will ultimately gain success in trading.

WHEN ENTERING A TRADE, INSTEAD OF ASKING HOW MUCH YOU CAN WIN, ASK YOURSELF HOW MUCH YOU CAN AFFORD TO LOSE. ALWAYS KEEP YOUR RISK MANAGEMENT IN CHECK!

Habit

Now that you understand the need to have a correct set of **values**, sufficient **knowledge** of the market, strategies, indicators as well as the **skills** to deploy them at your disposition, it is a matter of making it a habit to practise them. Once you have practised long enough to convert values, knowledge, and skills into habit, the rest becomes second nature to you (see Figure 2-1). Trust me, you will do what is right without even thinking about it!

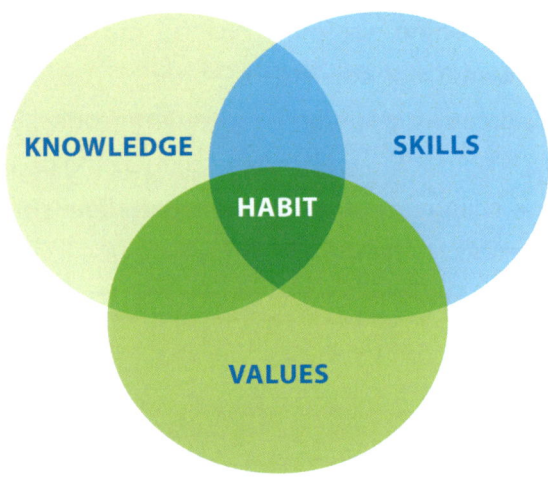

Figure 2-1: Habit = Practice (Knowledge + Values + Skill)

Too many traders simply do not practise long enough due to lack of determination or other "external" factors. The fault or problem always lies in other factors instead of themselves. Continue to think this way if you wish to remain as a non-profitable trader.

If you wish to be profitable in trading in the long run, do heed my advice—define your set of trading values, then devote time to gain knowledge on the market, the indicators, and strategies that you use. Do not forget about gaining knowledge by knowing more about yourself through trading journals (I will discuss this in Part 2) and convert what you learnt into trading skills. Keep practising them until they become second nature to you. This is the fastest way to be successful traders.

Have the patience to finish this book. I am sure you will pick up many important ideas and pointers, which will be useful to you in your trading journey. I will share with you various proven winning strategies I use, encompassing key trading psychology. The content in this book will fill in the knowledge and value portion, while the exercises will address the skills. As for habit, it all depends on you. Ask yourself this, "Do you want to be a profitable trader?"

Learning Points

- There are two hands of trading: the left is Probability of Win and the right is the Payoff Ratio.

- Take care of the downside and the upside will take care of itself.

- Focus on **being** a good trader, rather than on how much money you are going to make.

- Success in trading is an effect of doing the right things repeatedly over a period of time.

- Failure is an opportunity to learn about yourself, your setup, and the market.

- To increase your success rate, you need to double your failure rate (Thomas J. Watson).

- Successful trading is not about making money but about treating trading like a job.

- You define what success means to you. Otherwise you may spend your whole life working according to others' definitions of success.

Exercise

- I set my goals, which helped me get out of my crisis and brought me to where I am now. Have you set your goals yet? Write them down now.

_____

_____

_____

_____

_____

_____

- With your goals identified, devise specific plans to attain them. (Your goals need not be related to trading.)

_____

_____

_____

_____

_____

_____

Part I

FIGHTING THE OUTER WAR

"He who knows when he can fight and when he cannot, will be victorious."
– Sun Tzu

You will not be able to make a wise decision if you do not know your enemy well. To win a war, you need to know your enemy. That will determine whether or not to fight.

3 | PRODUCTS

When you are ready to put your money into the market, you should know what the available products are. More importantly, you ought to know which are most suitable for you and your risk appetite. I know too many people who wished to grow their money by investing and/or trading the market. However, they did not have a sound knowledge of the various products or investment vehicles available. This is the last thing I wish for my students and readers to encounter.

Knowing your choices and having a good knowledge of the products available are extremely important. Do not be ruled by the greed of wanting to make quick profits in the shortest time. To make money work for you, you must do your due diligence and work on your knowledge.

EDUCATION GIVES YOU THE HIGHEST FORM OF LEVERAGE

I will split products into three broad sectors: **Savings, Investment,** and **Trading**. I believe in diversifying my money among these three different sectors for a "whole-round" coverage. Although the risks and returns vary for different sectors, they average up to become a good plan for me in the long run. I hope you will benefit from what I will be sharing and will be able to make better decisions with your hard-earned money.

This chapter is dedicated to discuss on the types of products available from the three different sectors and which are the ones I buy, so as to build my wealth in both the short and long terms.

Savings

When talking about savings, the first thing that comes to your mind is likely bank savings or Fixed Deposits. Going by the interest rates offered by the banks nowadays (Table 3-1), growing your wealth this way seems to be hopeless. Have I mentioned inflation? I agree that depositing money into a bank is safe (almost), but in the long run, you lose money if you consider the effect of inflation. Now, is it still safe? Think again!

Bank	Amount (SGD)	6 mth (%)	12 mth (%)	24 mth (%)
Bank of China	10k-<50k	0.48	0.98	1.18
	50k-<200k	0.58	1.08	1.28
	>200k	0.68	1.18	1.38
CIMB	25-1 million	0.65	1.1	-
Citibank	>10k	0.1	0.1	0.1
DBS	1k-1 million	0.15	0.25	0.55
Hong Leong Finance	30k-<100k	-	1.05	1.18
	100-<200k	-	1.1	1.23
	>200k	-	1.15	1.28
HSBC	5k-1 million	0.13	0.19	0.25
Maybank	1k-<250k	0.4	0.7	0.9
	250k-1 million	1	1	1.1
OCBC	5k-<20k	0.15	0.25	0.55
	>20k-1 million	0.15	1 (Promo)	0.55
Standard Chartered (Step-Up Time Deposit)	>10k	1.08	1.18	1.38
UOB	>5k-1 million	0.15	1 (13 mths min 20k)	0.55

Table 3-1: Bank interest rates (estimated) as of May 2014 (Source: cheaponana.com)

For savings, other products we are more familiar with are mainly insurance products such Endowment Policy, Whole Life, and Term Policy.

In the past, when buying insurance, all the money goes into the insurance company in the first year. The money is used to pay the financial adviser, company shareholders, administrative fees, etc. Basically, no money goes back to you despite having paid so much for the premium. The situation is better now as some money goes back to you in the first year.

The most common insurance product is the Endowment Policy, in which the insurance company added an investment component to a Term Policy. Usually, the insurance company does the investing under their company's account with your premium. With this, it is tough for you to keep track on the Return of Investment (ROI). If the investment did make money, you, the insured will only get a small portion of the returns from investment. It is a no brainer that the insurance company is the one that benefits most.

I will take this chance to introduce a concept called "**Buy Term Invest the Difference**". This is not widely known or used because it is not profitable for insurance companies. The commission is not attractive enough for the agent as well as the insurance company. This explains why it is not aggressively promoted by most insurance companies.

Buying a Term Policy costs you less compared to paying for an Endowment Policy with **similar coverage**. With the balance of money saved, you can invest it in the stock market yourself. A Term Policy is not only cheaper compared to other insurance plans; it is also more liquid, which means you can sell it anytime you want, instead of waiting for maturity.

For example, you pay $1,000 a month to an insurance company for an Endowment Policy. Part of the money you pay is to insure yourself; the bigger portion is to be invested under the insurance company's account. As mentioned earlier, winnings from the investment are tough for you to track. Rest assured that most of the winnings go back to the insurance company. Buying a Term Policy costs you much less, say $100. This is because it purely insures you and does not have an investment component that Endowment Policies do. You can then invest the balance of $900 directly into the stock market yourself. Therefore, instead of paying $1,000 for an Endowment Policy, you can get a Term Policy (offering similar coverage) for $100 and invest the balance $900 into stock market, offering much more visibility to you.

The problem is most do not know how and where to invest this money. Quite a handful want to invest the money in the stock market, but they do not know when to enter the market. One option you can consider is the Share Builder Plan (SBP). SBP is an investment cum savings plan offered by Phillip Securities. It is a plan that allows you to buy stocks at a regular basis by using a technique known as **Dollar Cost Average**. With this technique, using the same amount of money, more shares are purchased when the prices of shares are low and fewer shares are purchased when the prices are high.

By investing a fixed amount of funds consistently every month over a period of time, your average cost of shares purchased will be lower, thus reducing the risk of investing a large amount in a single investment at the wrong time. This technique is good for investors who are not good at timing the market.

Table 3-2 illustrates the advantage of Dollar Cost Averaging.

| THE ADVANTAGE OF DOLLAR COST AVERAGING | | | | | |
| (based on a hypothetical investment of $100 per month) | | | | | |
Month	Share Price	Shares Bought	Portfolio Worth	Total Investment	Net Gain/Loss
1	$20	5.00	$100	$100	0.00%
2	$18	5.56	$190	$200	-5.00%
3	$16	6.25	$269	$300	-10.37%
4	$14	7.14	$335	$400	-16.18%
5	$12	8.33	$387	$500	-22.52%
6	$10	10.00	$423	$600	-29.53%
7	$13	7.69	$650	$700	-7.19%
8	$15	6.67	$850	$800	6.20%
9	$14	7.14	$893	$900	-0.78%
10	$17	5.88	$1,184	$1,000	18.43%
11	$19	5.26	$1,424	$1,100	29.42%
12	$20	5.00	$1,599	$1,200	33.22%

Table 3-2: Example of dollar cost averaging

For example:

Month 1 – Price is high and you buy fewer shares.

Month 2 – Price drops and you are able to buy more shares with the same amount of money invested.

Month 3 – Price drops further and you are able to buy even more shares with the same amount of money invested.

This goes on. Look at the Net Gain/Loss at the end of the year in Table 3-2.

SBP is most suitable for:

- Fresh graduates who have just joined the workforce.
- Those without significant capital or savings.
- Investors who are interested in long-term investment.

Through "Buy Term Invest the Difference", with the same amount of money spent (compared to buying an Endowment Policy), you get insured (with similar coverage as a typical Endowment Policy) and at the same time get more returns from investments through SBP in the long run. One more advantage of SBP is that only handling fees are incurred and this is a considerably small sum. There is no brokerage or front-end load when you purchase shares through SBP.

For me, where savings are concerned, this is what I do personally. Remember: I am thinking very long term with this, and this is why I define it as savings.

Example of "Buy Term Invest the Difference"

Let me give you a live example so that it is easier for you to understand, relate, and realise the power of this strategy.

Table 3-3 is extracted from an insurance company and let us call it insurance company P.

End of Policy Year/Age	Total Premiums Paid To-date ($)	Guaranteed ($)	Non-Guaranteed ($)	Total ($)
DEATH BENEFIT (3.25% investment return per year)				
1/31	3,617	100,000	0	100,000
2/32	7,234	100,000	0	100,000
3/33	10,851	100,000	1,004	101,004
4/34	14,468	100,000	2,085	102,085
5/35	18,085	100,000	3,301	103,301
6/36	21,702	100,000	4,635	104,635
7/37	25,319	100,000	6,154	106,154
8/38	28,936	100,000	7,823	107,823
9/39	32,553	100,000	9,237	109,237
10/40	36,170	100,000	10,684	110,684
15/45	54,255	100,000	18,435	118,435
20/50	72,340	100,000	26,720	126,724
25/55	90,425	100,000	35,417	135,417
30/60	108,510	100,000	56,354	156,354

Table 3-3: Example of endowment insurance plan

The table shows an Endowment Insurance Plan from P. The insured is assumed to be 30 years of age (male/non-smoker). The insurance policy term is 30 years with a yearly premium of $3,617.

For example, if the insured passes away at the age of 40, the premium paid thus far is $36,170. Upon death, the insured is guaranteed $100,000 with a non-guaranteed investment return of $10,684. As such, the total return would be $110,684.

If the insured passes away at the age of 60 or upon maturity of policy, he/she will get back $156,354 in total, after paying a total premium of $108,510. The insured ROI (return on investment) is about 44%.

Table 3-4 indicates what the insured will get if he/she chooses to give up the policy. For example, if the insured wishes to give up the policy at the age of 50, he/she will have paid a total premium of $72,340. The insured's guaranteed and non-guaranteed returns will be $53,957 and $10,092 respectively (assuming 3.25% investment return per year). His/her total returns will be only $64,049, running a loss!

SURRENDER VALUE (3.25% investment return per year)				
End of Policy Year/Age	Total Premiums Paid To-date ($)	Guaranteed ($)	Non-Guaranteed ($)	Total ($)
1/31	3,617	0	0	0
2/32	7,234	0	0	0
3/33	10,851	4,197	249	4,446
4/34	14,468	6,406	521	6,927
5/35	18,085	8,692	816	9,508
6/36	21,702	11,057	1,138	12,195
7/37	25,319	13,502	1,489	14,991
8/38	28,936	16,029	1,872	17,901
9/39	32,553	18,642	2,285	20,927
10/40	36,170	21,342	2,732	24,074
15/45	54,255	36,279	5,623	41,902
20/50	72,340	53,957	10,092	64,049
25/55	90,425	74,923	17,842	92,765

Table 3-4: Example of endowment insurance plan

Now, let's assume that the insured adopts a "Buy Term Invest the Difference" approach. From the same company P, the sum assured is still $100,000 upon death, with a yearly premium of only $266 (Table 3-5).

End of Policy Year/Age	Total Premiums Paid ($)	Guaranteed Death Benefit
1/31	266	100,000
2/32	532	100,000
3/33	798	100,000
4/34	1,064	100,000
5/35	1,330	100,000
6/36	1,596	100,000
7/37	1,862	100,000
8/38	2,128	100,000
9/39	2,394	100,000
10/40	2,660	100,000
15/45	3,990	100,000
20/50	5,320	100,000
25/55	6,650	100,000
30/60	7,980	100,000

Table 3-5: Example of Term Policy

Instead of paying $3,617 yearly to company P for an Endowment Policy, you pay only $266 per year for a Term Policy. You can invest the balance of $3,351 in the stock market. From many open literature, the average annual returns (inclusive of dividends) for Straits Times Index (STI) in general is about 9.5%.

If you invest $3,351 yearly in the STI, you could potentially gain $506,004 (round numbers) in returns after 30 years (not forgetting the power of compound interest) (Table 3-6).

Year	Estimated Investment Returns ($)
1	3,669 (3,351 + 9.5%)
2	7,368 [(3,669 + 9.5%) + 3,351)
3	11,418 [(7,368 + 9.5%) + 3351]
4	15,853
5	20,710
6	26,029
7	31,853
8	38,230
9	45,213
10	52,859
11	61,231
12	70,399
13	80,438
14	91,431
15	103,468
16	116,649
17	131,081
18	146,885
19	164,190
20	183,139
21	203,889
22	226,609
23	251,488
24	278,730
25	308,561
26	341,225
27	376,993
28	416,158
29	459,044
30	506,004

Table 3-6: Example of annual returns from STI

At the end of 30 years, your Term Policy would be rendered useless and you would have lost $7,980 in total. Despite losing $7,980, with your gain of $506,004 from the stock market your ROI after 30 years would be 336%!

You can see the summary in Table 3-7 for a better understanding.

	Endowment Insurance Plan	Buy Term Invest the Difference
Coverage	$100,000	$100,000
Total amount invested in insurance (30 years to maturity)	$108,510 ($3,617 x 30 years)	$7,980 ($266 x 30 years)
Amount invested in stock market annually	$0	$3,351
Net amount invested in stock market in 30 years	$0	$100,530 ($3,351 x 30 years)
Total returns	$156,354	$506,004
Total profit (after 30 years)	$47,844 ($156,354 - $108,510)	$397,494 ($506,004 - $7,980 - $100,530)
Total return of investment (after 30 years)	44%	366%

Table 3-7: Summary of differences between "Buy Term Invest the Difference" and a typical Endowment Policy

Investment

Investing is one of the important vehicles you need to build your wealth. Investing is more for the mid to long term—that is two years or more. Exchange-Traded Funds (ETF) and Unit Trusts are two of the products many people use for investing.

ETFs are open-ended investment funds listed and traded on a stock exchange. They aim to track, replicate or correspond to the performance of an underlying index or asset. ETFs provide access to a wide variety of markets as well as asset classes and similar to trading any stock, you may buy or sell ETFs through your stock broker or through your own online trading account. ETFs are actually very similar to Unit Trusts. The only major difference is that there are no performance fees with ETFs. Investors therefore pay lower management fees compared to hefty fees paid to fund managers when buying Unit Trusts.

When you buy a Unit Trust, you need to pay the fund manager a management fee regardless of whether you are winning money or not. This fund manager is the one who manages your account and money. As professionals, we trust that they can make better buy or sell judgments than us and eventually provide us with sound advice, with the aim of making more money for us compared to doing the investing ourselves. If you do not mind the hefty fees and are clueless about the market, Unit Trusts may be one of the products you want to consider.

Investing my money into ETFs is my preferred choice due to its very low management fees and other advantages depicted in Table 3-8.

	ETFs	Shares	Unit Trusts
Diversification	Yes	No	Yes
Price Transparency	Yes	Yes	No
Intra-day Trading	Yes	Yes	No
Sales Charges	None^	None^	3 - 5%
Management Fees	Less than 1%	None	1 - 2%
Dividend*	Yes	Yes	Yes
Traded through a broker	Yes	Yes	No
Cash Settlement	3rd business day after trade date	3rd business day after trade date	Upfront

*Subject to the discretion of the Fund Manager
^Usual brokerage commissions apply

Table 3-8: Comparison of the ETFs, Shares, and Unit Trusts in Singapore

Buying ETFs largely depends on the components of the particular ETF you buy, rather than the skill of a Fund Manager. This is the main reason why fees for Fund Managers are much lower. On top of that, due to how ETFs are structured, you can achieve diversification of an index fund through a single investment.

Do you know according to statistics, close to 70% of ETFs beat Unit Trusts in terms of returns ? One of the key reasons is due to the very low management fees involved when buying ETFs, as compared to high management fees paid to Unit Trusts Fund Managers. Nevertheless, sales agents still push for Unit Trusts as it offers them higher commissions as compared to buying ETFs, which is mostly done through an online platform.

Overall, I strongly recommend putting money into ETFs instead of Unit Trusts for long-term investments.

Trading

When it comes to trading, I am talking about a much shorter time frame in which a position would be closed within five trading days. Although what is discussed here is more applicable to the Singapore context, the principle can be applied in any market of most countries.

I use Contract for Difference (CFD) for trading. CFD is an agreement between two parties to settle the difference between the opening and closing prices of the contract multiplied by the number of units of the underlying asset specified in the CFD. CFDs allow customers to participate in the price movement of an underlying product without actually owning the asset, which may be a share, an index, a commodity, etc. Due to its versatility, I prefer to trade CFDs.

There are many types of CFD available, including Shares CFD, Direct Market Access (DMA) CFD, and World Indices CFD.

These are some benefits of trading CFD:
- "Short-sell" without hassle
- 20 times the investment power (for products under Phillip Securities)
- Sophisticated trading strategies (recommended for advance traders only)
- Real-time access to global markets through single trading platform

- No account maintenance fees
- Unlike Options, CFDs do not have expiry date and hence, have no price decay
- Minimum contract sizes (possible to buy one share)

Table 3-9 gives you a better overview on the key difference between stocks and CFD. For CFD, I use STI SGD5 as an example.

	Stocks	CFD Index (STI SGD5 CFD)
Transaction Cost	0.25%	0.03%
Exchange Fees	0.005%	NA
Leverage	NIL	20 times
Short Sell	No	Yes
Suspend	Yes	No
Spread	0.005	0.0013

Table 3-9: Comparison table between stocks and STI SGD5 CFD

Of course, although the CFD is my preferred choice, it is not without its drawback. CFD is traded Over-The-Counter (OTC), which means trading financial instruments such as stocks, bonds, commodities or derivatives directly between two parties. Buying and selling directly from banks or market-makers means your money will be at risk if the bank from which you bought the CFD folds or collapses.

Do note that different types of CFDs come with different commission fees and different leverages. Please do your due diligence on the costs involved and check with your broker if you are unsure. Do note that the World Indices CFD is a highly leveraged trading instrument and you can lose more than what you put in!

TRADING IS LIKE RUNNING ANY OTHER BUSINESS. YOU HAVE TO STUDY THE RISKS AND COSTS INVOLVED IN RUNNING YOUR TRADING BUSINESS

Conclusion

In this chapter, I shared with you the products I bought in the three different sectors: savings, investing, and trading. It is a good idea to diversify your money, buying products that benefit you most for each sector. This puts your money into different baskets, spreading your risk while obtaining "whole-round" coverage.

It is unwise to put all your money into one risky component hoping to make a big quick buck in the shortest possible time. Many have tried to do this. Only a few got lucky once or twice. Thus, I cannot stress any more the importance of understanding the products available and which are most suitable for you in the three different sectors. Remember, if you wish to build your wealth, you ought to do your due diligence. With this book as your starting point, build your knowledge by doing more research to understand what you are buying to trade and invest.

SUCCESS DOES NOT COME EASY AND THERE ARE NO SHORT CUTS!

Learning Points

- Put your money in the three different sectors of savings, investing, and trading so as make them work harder for you.

- Money will not work for you, if you do not put in your due diligence.

- Know your products well and do your research before committing the money. Do not be greedy or impatient.

- When it comes to insurance, buy term and invest the difference.

- The more structured the product, the higher the cost.

- Knowing the difference between the trader and investor is essential. It determines which strategies to adopt.

- There is no quick fix in the stock market. Do not bet all your money on one product.

Exercise

- What products will you use for:
  a. Savings

  _____

  _____

  b. Investment

  _____

  _____

  c. Trading

  _____

  _____

- What are your plans for:
  a. Saving

  _____

  _____

  b. Investment

  _____

  _____

  c. Trading

  _____

  _____

4 | TRADERSGPS SYSTEM

rading using technical indicators is like using the map and compass. System trading is like using a GPS. The challenge in system trading is most people do not have the experience, time and money to learn how to do it effectively. For a GPS to work, it must be tested for accuracy and reliability. This is the same for TradersGPS. System trading came to me because of necessity as I did not deliberately plan to go into system trading. It was during that time when I could not trade full time after my client lost the $250,000 that I realised the need to trade longer term and to systemise my trading. The TradersGPS system is thus born out of desperation and necessity.

When it comes to position trading, you want to always ride the trend until it changes. In position trading, positions are open or closed for two weeks or longer, depending on the progress and the current state of the trend. Most position traders use longer time frame charts with daily, weekly or even monthly candlesticks. This style of trading suits most long-term investors or traders who only have time to monitor their trades once a day. This is ideal for traders who are holding a full-time job.

I like to "scale in" for position trading. This means entering more lots at the earlier part of the trend when it is still building and slowly decrease lots to enter as it progresses to maturity. We must always remember that trends do not only go in one direction. They can change anytime. Hence, it is our duty to watch them closely.

ADD POSITION WHEN YOU ARE RIGHT, CUT LOSS QUICKLY WHEN YOU ARE WRONG

BUY MORE WHEN I AM RIGHT, SELL FAST WHEN I AM WRONG

For long term trading like position trading, I prefer developing systems to mechanise my entries and exits. That means entries and exits are performed by the computer without human intervention. This greatly reduces the involvement of emotions, which complicates the already complex equation of trading. This system will also help take care and to calculate proper position sizing (to be discussed in later chapter) for every trade made. This ensures that my trading account will remain healthy, even when suffering a series of losses. With a system, the trading process will be systemised and therefore eliminating discretions.

Discretionary Trading (Map and Compass) and Mechanical Trading (GPS)

There are two types of trading: discretionary and mechanical trading.

Mechanical trading is based on parameters historically validated by back-testing quantifiable market data. Once the entry and exit criteria have been defined, the trader should follow the signals exactly.

Discretionary trading is a process of entering and exiting a trade based on feeling or "gut feel". The most common form of discretionary trading is a concept called "tape reading". According to the website *Investopedia*, tape reading is an old investing technique used by day traders to analyse the price and volume of a particular stock to execute profitable trades.

Personally, I prefer mechanical to discretionary trading, as I like to have a set of rules and guidelines to define and guide my entry and exit criteria.

TradersGPS System

In this chapter, I will introduce **TradersGPS System**. This is a system which I invented and it is still one of my favourite and most profitable trading systems. Nevertheless, in any system you use, make sure you perform a stock selection check to affirm the stocks you trade follow the system's rules and strategies. You can easily do so by back-testing it. Do not be so confident about your system that you skip the back-testing process. As a trader, you must bear in mind that different stocks behave differently, like human beings. There is no one strategy that suits all stocks. This is the reason I do not believe in a "holy grail" system or strategy.

Before moving on, I want to emphasise that this chapter is not to show how powerful the TradersGPS is. Rather, it is to share with you how I read the market, understand each and every oscillator, and designed the system based on factors and parameters that have worked for me. You may wish to design your own system based on your own understanding, habits, and studies of the market. That way, you can adjust your system or parameters to suit the ever-changing conditions of the market.

The market usually presents three different trends: long-term, intermediate-term, and short-term trends. With the TradersGPS, I break up the three trends into in-depth studies before making any buy or sell decisions. In this system, I name the three trends: tide (long-term), wave (intermediate-term), and ripple (short-term). I will share more details shortly.

The TradersGPS System runs on the ChartNexus platform, a commercial platform which you can easily download from the official website. Figure 4-1 shows how a ChartNexus platform looks like.

Figure 4-1: An example of a ChartNexus chart

Let us drill deeper into the trading system so that you can have a better understanding of how it works and more importantly, how I derived it. It is crucial for traders to understand their systems before using them! Only then can you tweak or modify your systems to suit your needs and crucially, adapt to changing market conditions. Remember that the market, like humans, do change.

Figure 4-2 shows how the TradersGPS System looks like in ChartNexus. Looking at the chart (APPL), you see a blue oscillator, which is what I call cumulation of momentum (COM). It uses the momentum of the long, mid, and short terms to determine the COM. It is beyond the scope of this book to cover how the COM is calculated. What is important is how I make use of it to read market trends and patterns.

Figure 4-2: TradersGPS System

COM of TradersGPS

- Bullish = COM above 0
- Bearish = COM below 0

If the COM is above 0, it indicates that the overall market is bullish. If the COM falls below 0, the market is bearish.

The gradient of the COM also tells another story (Figure 4-3). It represents the strength of the tide. When it is in the bullish section (above 0) with positive gradient, it indicates bullishness. The steeper the gradient, the more bullish the tide is. If the gradient is negative in the bullish section, it is telling me that the bullish tide is losing strength. I will interpret it as having to get ready to exit my long positions.

When COM is in the bearish section with negative gradient, it indicates bearishness. The steeper the gradient, the more bearish the tide is. On the other hand if the gradient is positive in the bearish section, it means the bearish tide is losing strength. That could mean getting prepared to exit my short position. When the trend of the stock price does not agree with the trend of the COM, a divergence occurs, signalling a possible trend reversal.

Figure 4-3: Reading the gradient of Insider Swing

Figure 4-4 is an example of a **bearish divergence** in which the indicator is making lower lows while the price is making higher highs. Notice after the divergence surfaces, the trend reverses into a bearish one. You may use it as an early warning signal to exit when you are in a long position.

Figure 4-4: Reading bearish divergence of COM

In a **bullish divergence** chart (Figure 4-5), the reverse is true. The price is making lower lows while the indicator is making higher highs. Subsequently, the price reverses into an uptrend. A bullish divergence gives me an early signal that a trend reversal may be on its way.

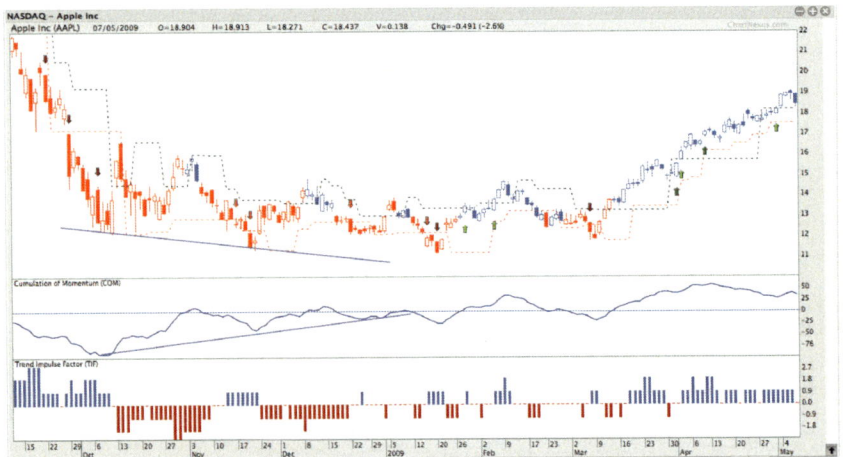

Figure 4-5: Reading bullish divergence of COM

Trend Impulse Factor

- Trend is strong = Trend Impulse Factor above 0
- Trend is weak = Trend Impulse Factor below 0

The TIF measures the strength of the trend. If it is below 0, the trend may be weak. If it is above 0, it indicates a strong trend (which could be either bullish or bearish).

Looking at Figure 4-6, when the signal to buy appears (green arrow) at #1, the TIF is above 0, which indicates bullish strength. This is a good opportunity to enter a long trade. Another signal to buy appears at #2; the TIF is above 0, which indicates strong bullish strength. This means another opportunity to enter a long trade. Bullish trend weakens so even though another signal to buy appear at #3, I may not add on to my existing long position #4, which shows a weakening uptrend.

Figure 4-6: Trend Impulse Factor (TIF) of the TradersGPS

The same explanation applies for bearish trades. Looking at Figure 4-7, an opportunity to enter a short trade arises when a red arrow appears. At this point, the TIF reads above 0, indicating a strong trend. The price continues dropping at #2 and #3; the TIF shows the trend continues to be strong. At #4, it is warning me that the strength of this downtrend is weakening. I may once again choose to stay away from shorting this stock. True enough, price continues sideways and eventually start to turn up.

Figure 4-7: Trend Impulse Factor (TIF) of the TradersGPS

The TIF helps me to "rank" the arrow: the higher the value, the more impulsive the arrow.

I will explain more on the arrows (entry signals) later in this chapter. As of now, simply take these as the signal to enter the market.

Peak and Trough Line

The Peak (resistance) and Trough (support) is what I call the PT Line, which I incorporate for more accurate entry and exit criteria. The red dotted line is the Trough Line; the black dotted line is the Peak Line.

PT Line
- Dotted red line = Trough Line (support)
- Dotted black line = Peak Line (resistance)

You can use the PT line as support and resistance and for putting in your trailing stops. Notice in Figure 4-8, the price is maintained above the dotted red line (Trough) until 21 May when the price closes below the Trough Line (Support). This signals you to close all your long (buy) positions.

Figure 4-8: Peak and Trough Line (PT Line) of TradersGPS

The same applies to short or bearish trades. Figure 4-9 shows many short opportunities, allowing me to make decent profits. On 28 February 2008, the price went up and closed above peak line (black), signalling me to exit all my short positions for a profit.

Figure 4-9: Peak and Trough line for entry and exit signals

Arrows

Two algorithms work behind the scenes for TradersGPS.

1. **Breakout method**: based on the PT line (breaking above the resistance or support).
2. **Retracement method**: based on the Market Cycle (the interplay of the tide, wave, and ripple).

Do note that once the arrows appear (Figure 4-10), you will buy one cent above the high of the candle where the arrow appears. In the event this does not happen, use the latest day high as the trigger to execute a long trade. The chart in Figure 4-11 further illustrates this.

Figure 4-10: Arrows of TradersGPS

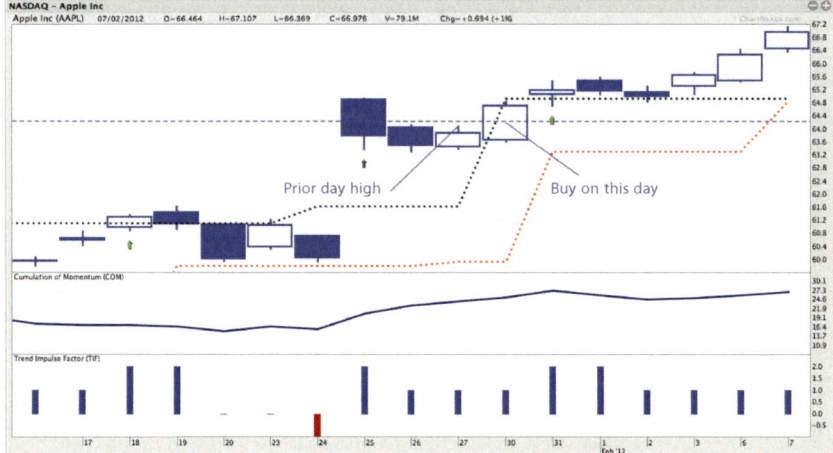

Figure 4-11: Arrows giving bullish entry signal

The same theory applies to bearish trades. Looking at Figure 4-12, a red arrow appears at #1, signalling a short opportunity. A red arrow appears at #2 when price breaks and closes below trough line, also signalling a short opportunity and, in this case, to add on to an existing short position.

Figure 4-12: Arrows giving the bearish entry signal

Do note that once the arrows appear, you will sell or short one cent below the low of the candle where the arrow appears. In event this does not happen, you will use the latest day low as the trigger to execute a short trade.

Putting Things Together

When using a system, not only should you understand how it works, it is also important that you follow the rules religiously. Many traders failed to allow the system to realise its own potential as they keep switching from one system to another after a few losing trades. Always remember that trading is nothing but a game of probability and there are bound to be losing trades, regardless of how powerful your systems or strategies are.

In summary, putting things together for the TradersGPS, you need all three signals to buy:

Buy

- COM above 0 (Blue Candle)
- Buy Arrow
- TIF above 0

Once these three signals are available:

- Trigger to buy 1 bid above the high of the trigger candle where the arrow appears or the high of following candle(s).

To exit long positions for cutting loss or profit taking:

- Wait for price to break and close below trough, or;
- Wait for candlestick to change from Blue to Red (COM below 0).

Similarly, you need all three signals to sell:

Sell

- COM below 0 (Red Candle)
- Sell Arrow
- TIF above 0

Once all three signals are available:

- Trigger to sell 1 bid below the low of the trigger bar where the arrow appears or the low of following candle(s).

To exit short positions for cutting loss or profit taking:

- Wait for price to break and close above peak, or;
- Wait for candlestick to change from red to blue;
- Break and close above peak coupled with a green arrow.

In Summary

Indicator	Representation	Colour
COM	Overall Trend	Blue
Peak Line	Resistance	Black Dotted
Trough	Support	Red Dotted
TIF	Strength	Blue or Red

Advantage of Scaling In

The common problem faced by most traders who fail is **overtrading**. This means they took a position too big for themselves to handle. One single trade can ruin the health of their trading account. I have mentioned many times that traders should understand that no matter how powerful their strategies are, they will have losing trades. As such, I cannot stress anymore the importance of position sizing and money management.

BUY MORE WHEN I AM RIGHT, CUT FAST WHEN I AM WRONG

For position sizing, I adopt the "Triangle" methodology (Figure 4-13).

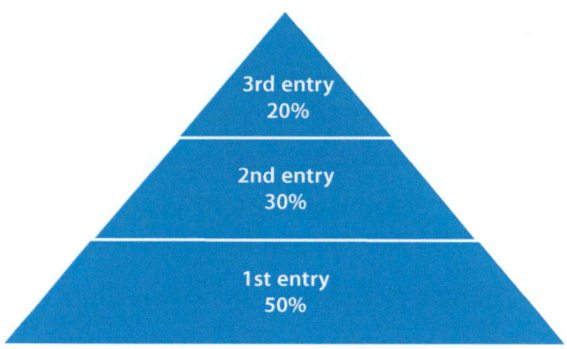

Figure 4-13: The "Triangle" methodology for position sizing

I discuss position sizing in later chapters. But the advantage of adopting this methodology is obvious. When a trend is forming, it may not be stable in the beginning. With 50% committed for a trade, your loss will be minimal in the event that your trade reverses, which is highly possible.

NOTHING IS GUARANTEED IN TRADING

As the trend matures, there may be a higher chance of it reversing, probably due to profit taking (or other unforeseeable market conditions). Thus, it is not a bad idea to enter a smaller percentage to keep loss and risk minimal. Even if the trend continues to progress, you are not denied the opportunity to ride it further, and hence, utilise the idea of scaling in.

The TradersGPS System allows traders to scale in their positions, so as to maximise profits as the trade progresses in their favour. In Figure 4-14, the first green arrow appears at #1 and I am 50% committed. At #2, another green arrow appears signalling me to add on to my positions, hence making me 80% committed. At #3, another green arrow appears and I can further scale in my positions, making me 100% committed. At #4, another entry opportunity arises; it is up to the traders if they wish to further scale in their position. While this example is for long or bullish trades, the same applies in short or bearish trades.

Figure 4-14: Scaling in positions using TradersGPS for bullish trades

Indicators and Oscillators in Your Systems

Even though the COM looks like it is only a single indicator, in actual case it is a set of three. I have simplified the decision-making process to make it easier for the end user.

I always have people asking me why am I using a set of oscillators to make entry and exit decisions, instead of just using one so as to simplify matters. In my opinion, there is a huge advantage in using a set of oscillators over just one. For example, if the big trend is giving a bullish signal while the medium trend gives a bearish signal, I know it is not timely to enter a trade yet and I shall wait. The overall picture is simply telling me a pullback is occurring while the underlying is still bullish. Shorting this stock may not be a good idea in this case, as the trend has yet to become my friend.

Of course, I am not asking traders to use so many oscillators that it clouds their vision. You may as well forget about trading as you will not have any entry opportunities. **It is important for traders to understand the purpose of particular oscillators or indicators and how they help you in your analysis.** In other words, understand the system you are using and how it works for you. By sharing with you my system, I hope you can understand my thought process better.

TradersGPS can minimise the whipsaws caused by ranging and false breakouts. Always remember that you need the tide, wave, and ripple to be aligned before making a trade. Thus, there will not be much buy or sell signals generated when the market is ranging as the tide, wave, and ripple conflict with one another.

Figures 4-15 represents a stock in consolidation with Moving Average Cross-over strategy. You will have many buy and sell signals and this can be painful if you are not able to cut loss when required to. With the TradersGPS, we only trade when the tide, wave, and ripple are telling the same story. That gives me more confidence each time a trade is made. No trades are made when the stock is in consolidation, hence minimising your risk and exposure to the market.

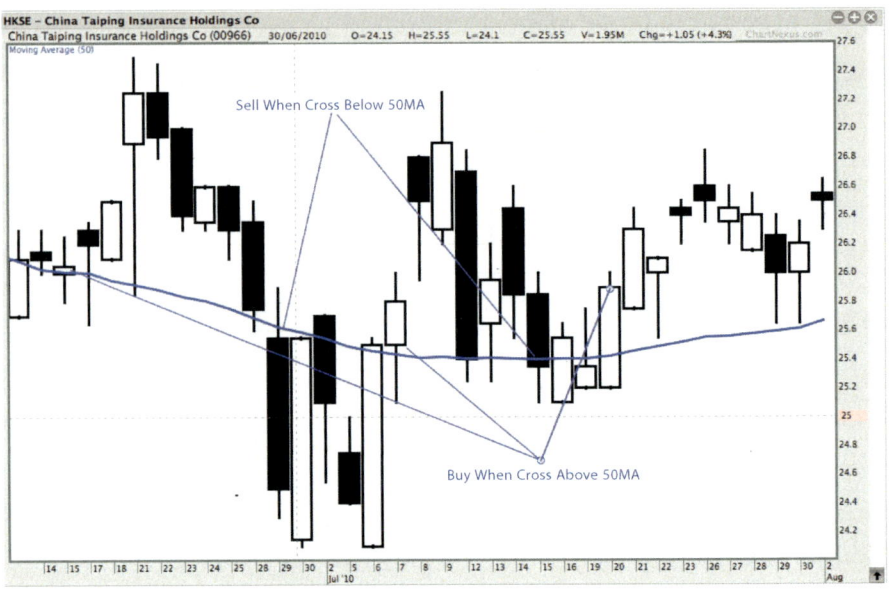

Figure 4-15: Example of a Moving Average Cross-over strategy

Conclusion

The most important takeaway is to understand your system (and every indicator and oscillator involved) so that you can adjust parameters to suit the ever changing market conditions. Remember, there is "no one size fits all" in trading. Do your due diligence and enjoy your fruits of labour thereafter.

Learning Points

- Buy more when you are right; sell fast when you are wrong.

- There are two types of trading: discretionary and mechanical. Identify which suits you better.

- The advantage of mechanical trading is the removal of emotions in trading.

- When the market goes up, it takes the stairs. When the market goes down, it takes the lift and sometimes even leaps off the building.

- There are three ways to use any oscillators: overbought or oversold, above or below the centre line, and divergence.

- There are at least three cycles happening on one stock. You need to know its tide, wave, and ripple.

- There are only three kinds of trading systems: trending, counter-trending, and volatility trading systems.

- Knowing the support and resistance is a vital skill in technical analysis.

Exercise

- What is your top takeaway from this chapter?

  Understand your System start
  with a few (no more than 3)
  indicators RSI, Delta, SMA,
  look for Convergence and
  Divergence   20%   Scale into
              30%,
         50%   position

- Do you have a system now? If your answer is yes, do you understand how it is designed? If not, how would you design your own?

  _____

  _____

  _____

  _____

  _____

5 SHORT-TERM TRADING STRATEGIES

I n this chapter, I will share with you some of my favourite winning strategies that I use. These strategies have been put through extensive back-testing and provided me with good returns in live trading all these years. I am sharing them with you so that you can focus on trading well, rather than engaging in an endless search for a "holy grail".

Different strategies suit different time frames. I believe there is no one-size-fits-all strategy.

There are a few factors to consider when you are deciding on your trading time frame:

- **Trading experience**
  The lesser the experience you have in trading, the longer the time frame you should choose. Trading intra-day charts (5 or 15 minutes) is the same as a daily chart. However, instead of

making one decision a day, you have to make a decision every 15 minutes.

- **Time**
  The lesser the time you have to devote to trading, the longer the time frame you should trade. If you are working full time, it makes no sense to trade intra-day as you need to be at your computer to watch your position, unless you are trading a market in a different time-zone such as the US.

- **Money**
  The lesser the money you can afford to lose, the longer your time horizon should be.

Most people are better off investing than trading in the long term, because of these three factors. However, for the few who aspire to trade full time, doing it part time first is the way to go. I strongly suggest getting a mentor if you aspire to go down this route. It is not an easy one. In a short while, I will show you another way with which you can still trade profitably with lesser experience, time and money, using a time-proven, back-tested trading system.

This is how I define my time frames (see Figure 5-1):
- **Intra-day trade**. Position opens and closes within the same trading day
- **Swing trade**. Position opens and closes within five trading days
- **Position trade**. Position opens and closes for two weeks or longer

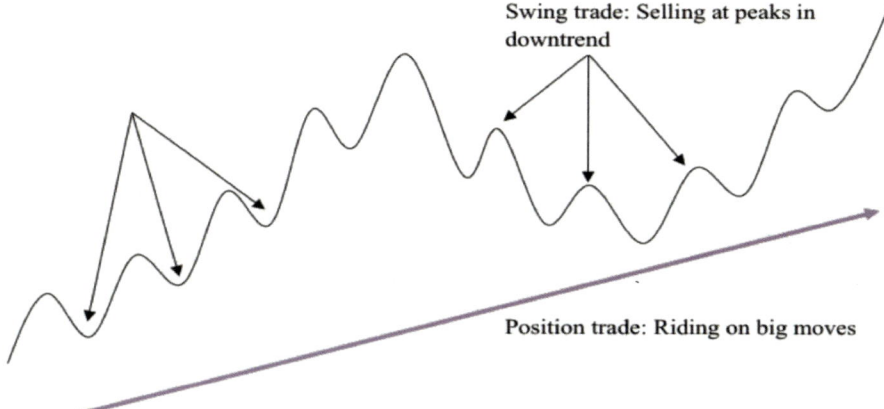

Figure 5-1: Illustration of position and swing trading

Intra-Day Trading

I do not do intra-day trading because trading is not my full-time job. It is not cost-effective for me to sit down in front of the computer to trade for long hours. When you trade in front of the computer, you are trading your time for money. However, what I have done, and am still doing, is algo trading, in which I programme the computer to trade on my behalf. Instead of working in the market, I work on the system that works on the market. That is how I leverage on technology to be more productive.

Swing Trading Strategy

For swing trading, the intention is to identify, follow, and trade the trend. Swing traders look to make profits within five trading days. Daily candles are frequently used for technical analysis, which determines the key entry and exit decisions in swing trading. For swing trades, traders generally buy the dips in an uptrend or sell the peak in a downtrend.

Remember the famous saying "*the trend is your friend*"? By trading the trend, you are riding the momentum of the market, which gives an edge to traders. It is like swimming with the current rather than against it. You should know how tough it is to swim against the current and eventually you will choose to give up due to exhaustion. Remember that as a trader, we must always have an edge over the market to be successful. This is just like a casino having an edge over the punters.

For new traders, you may not understand exactly what up and down trends are. To qualify as an uptrend, we look for higher highs and higher lows (Figure 5-2).

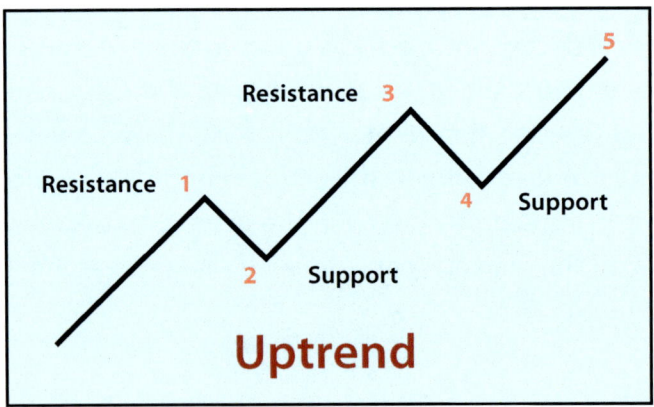

Figure 5-2: Illustration of market in uptrend

On the other hand, to qualify as a downtrend, we look for lower highs and lower lows (Figure 5-3).

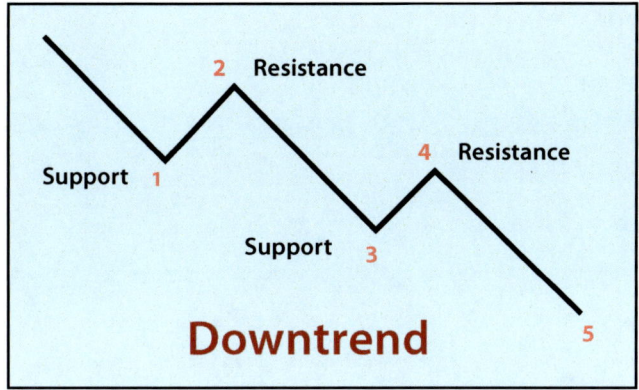

Figure 5-3: Illustration of market in downtrend

There are times when there are no higher highs or lower lows. Under such situations, the market is moving sideways, otherwise known as consolidation (Figure 5-4).

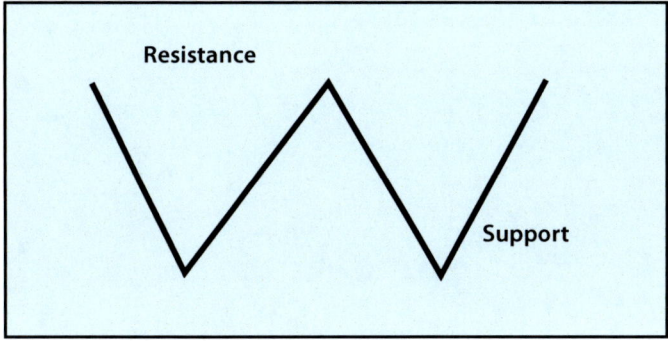

Figure 5-4: Illustration of market in consolidation

For trend trading, you have to identify two things:

- Current trend, which I call **tide** (Figure 5-5).
- Dips in an uptrend and rally in a downtrend, which I call **wave** (Figure 5-6).

Figure 5-5: Illustration of tides

Figure 5-6a: Illustration of waves

Figure 5-6b: Illustration of waves

I am using Simple Moving Average (SMA) to help read and identify trends (Figure 5-7). The parameters I frequently use are 20 and 40. A Moving Average (MA) is the average value of a security's price over a set period.

Figure 5-7: Identify market trends using moving averages

The parameters used for Moving Averages often mean something to certain individuals or institutions. 20 SMA, a trader's most dominant MA, can be used in all time frames. 50 SMA, mostly used by banks and institutions, is typically used on a daily time frame. Some traders use 50 SMA and 40 SMA interchangeably. It is up to individual preference. What many call the investor line, 200 SMA serves as a good support and resistance especially on 15-minute charts.

- 10 or 20 SMA – Traders' Line
- 40 or 50 SMA – Banks and Institutions' Line
- 200 SMA – Investors' Line

Based on my experience, it is not the number or parameter you use on your charts. Rather, it is how you use or perceive it in accordance with your trading strategy. Some traders like to use 21 SMA as 21 is a Fibonacci number. To them, they may have a good understanding of Fibonacci numbers and believe that the number 21 means something in the equity market. To me, it does not really matter if the number is 20, 21 or 19. Once again, it is how I interpret the number, what it means to me, and how I use it to define my setups. So do not be too concerned with precisely which number to use, dwelling on endless research for the "holy number".

There are many ways to use MAs. For example, many traders use MAs for crossover setups or to analyse a trend (Figure 5-8).

For me however, I do not use it as a signal to buy or sell. Instead, the gradient of the MA gives an analysis of the strength of a trend. If 200 SMA is sloping up, it is telling me that long-term investors are bullish about that particular stock. With 20 SMA sloping up, it is telling me that the short-term traders are bullish about the stock. If 20 SMA is sloping up, 50 SMA is flat while 200 SMA is sloping down, it is telling me that the short-term traders are bullish, the banks are neutral while the investors are bearish about the stock. The chart must be able to tell us a story. This story told helps traders like us make better decisions.

Figure 5-8: Crossover setups

Aside from the slope, you can inspect the sequence of the MAs. A bullish trend is considered established when 200, 50, and 20 MAs are aligned respectively as shown in Figure 5-9. The opposite is true for bearish trends.

Figure 5-9: Alignment of Moving Averages to determine market trend

If the sequence of the MAs is 50, 20, and 200 respectively, a trend is yet to be established. You may wish to stay at the sideline while waiting for an opportunity. Do not be too eager to enter a trade when the signal to enter is not shown.

Studying the space between the MAs is another option. If the MAs are far apart, it acts as an "insulator", which also means that the current trend is very strong. Under such conditions, when the price drops into the MAs, it will likely bounce off and resume its prior trend (Figure 5-10).

Figure 5-10: Determine strong market strength using Moving Averages

In contrast, if the MAs are narrow, it may signify that the trend is weak and a change in trend may occur (Figure 5-11). Hence, you have to be cautious when entering a trade under such conditions.

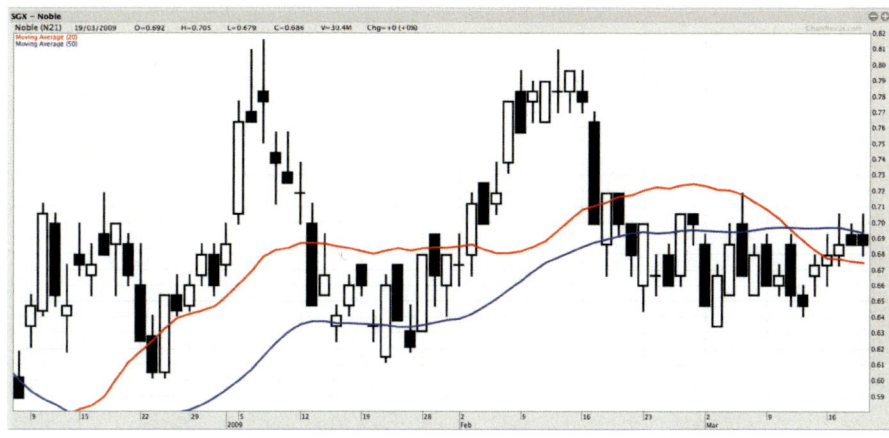

Figure 5-11: Determine weak market strength using Moving Averages

Personally, I feel it is not good enough to just identify tides as we may end up buying the top of an uptrend or selling at the bottom of a downtrend. As such, we should always aim to buy a dip or pullback in an uptrend and to sell a rally in a downtrend.

I use CCI (5) to effectively identify a dip (in an uptrend) or rally (in a downtrend). Basically, CCI measures the current price level relative to an average price level over a given period of time, which in my case is five days. CCI is relatively high when prices are far above their average. CCI is relatively low when prices are far below their average. In this manner, CCI can be used to identify overbought and oversold levels.

The reason why I use CCI as compared to momentum indicators (which is frequently used by many other traders) is that the latter takes only two points to compute the value. Momentum and rate of change (ROC) are simple technical analysis indicators displaying the difference between today's closing price and the close N-days ago. With that, it is evident to me that CCI provides more stories about the market, as it takes into account the values for every past N-day. This will make a big difference in your studies, especially when you look at the shorter term.

I use "5" as my parameter in CCI because the equity market has a certain pattern that repeats itself. Generally, the uptrend market has around five to seven candles up followed by three candles down, and vice versa for a downtrend. If the tide is up, three candles going up, and five to seven candles down, it may signal a reverse in trend. Also, not to forget, there are five trading days in a week; traders like to open their position at the beginning of the week and close trades before the end of the week. Thus, as compared to other numbers, using 5 as my CCI parameter resonates with me better. Of course, you can have another set of numbers that suit your own strategies.

CCI will generally oscillate between overbought (+100) and oversold (-100). We will study it closely to observe how the price has pulled back.

Look at Figure 5-12. I describe my setup for a **Bullish Swing Trade**.

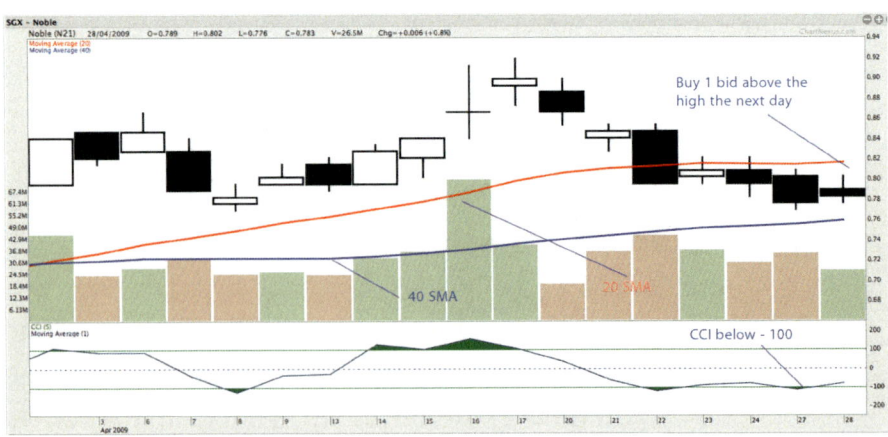

Figure 5-12a: Example of bullish swing trade

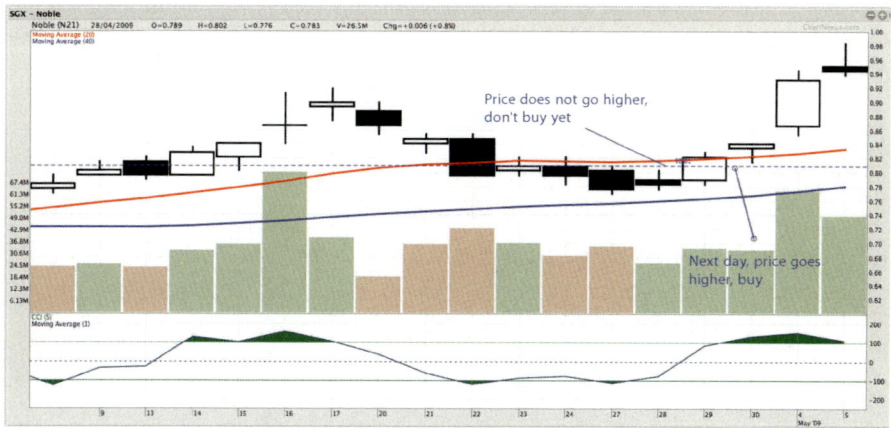

Figure 5-12b: Example of bullish swing trade

- 20 MA and 40 MA must be sloping up (with 20 MA above 40 MA). Having a space between the MAs further indicates the strength of the trend.

- Wait for the price to pull back to 20 SMA. Take note that during very bullish or bearish situations, the price may pull back to 10 SMA only, not to 20 SMA. Thus, we need to be flexible at times as trading is an art, not just a science. If the price pulls back to 10 SMA and CCI is at -100, it is still a possible setup.

- Look out for meaningful pullbacks to buy on a dip, which means we must wait for CCI be at -100.

- Next, look for the buy zone, which is the region between 20 and 40 MA. When the price is inside this zone, it means we have to get ready to enter a trade. It is important that we do not hesitate.

- Buy when the price trades 1 bid above previous day's high. The high of previous candle is the most bullish point for previous day. If today's high can conquer the previous day's high, it means today is more bullish. (At this time, your CCI need not necessarily be at -100, but it should have visited -100 before.)

- Stop-loss at 1 bid below previous day low or today's low, whichever is lower.

For any strategy, traders must always look out for a Payoff Ratio of more than 1 before entering a trade. That means the amount of potential profit made must be more than what you would potentially lose if the trade went sour. More on Payoff Ratio will be shared in a later chapter.

For this swing trading strategy, we always buy at the point where the price has made a pullback after a bull run, where we believe that the trend will continue thereafter. Before taking the trade, we identify the previous high as our profit target, and the previous day or today's low as our risk (stop-loss). With that, we calculate the Payoff Ratio. The general rule of thumb is to have the Payoff Ratio to be 2, or at least 1. Having a Payoff Ratio of 2 simply means that if the trade is a winning one, we will make $100 (for example), or if it happens to be a losing trade, we will lose $50.

In general, ensure that what you are likely to win is going to be more than what you are likely to lose if the trade happened to be a losing one. Couple this with a strategy with Probability of Win of at least 0.5 and you will definitely be profitable in the long run when you do the math. More on Probability of Win will be discussed later in this chapter.

Sometimes, the price can be so bullish that the CCI did not pull back to the oversold region, but to the neutral region (at 0). You can still enter such trades under such circumstances. It is optional; you can still make the trade depending on your comfort level and experience. I know we are always looking for ideal setup conditions to be sure that the trade will make you money. But you will not always see textbook situations in the stock markets. Even if the setup is ideal, it does not mean this trade will definitely be a winning one. Whatever your decision is, never fail to ask yourself what the Payoff Ratio is before making a trade.

For this strategy, the opposite applies for bearish trades (Figure 5-13).

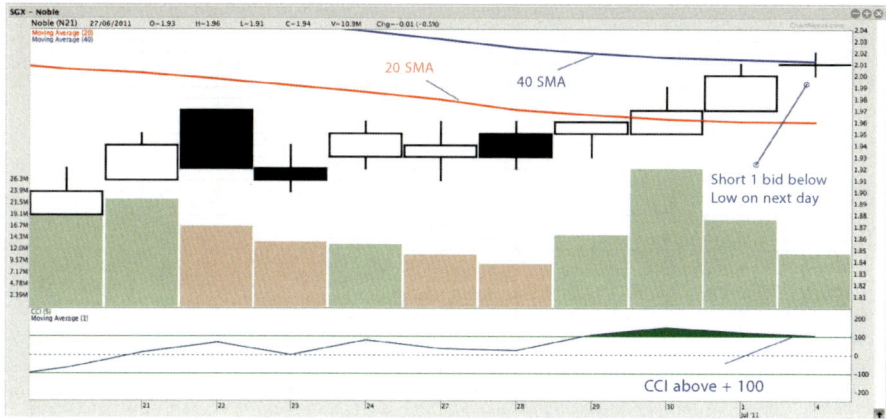

Figure 5-13a: Example of bearish swing trade

Figure 5-13b: Example of bearish swing trade

For a summary of the Swing Trading Setups we have discussed, see Table 5-1.

Bullish Setup	Bearish Setup
1. Sloping up Moving Average	1. Sloping down Moving Average
2. 20 MA above 40MA	2. 20 MA below 40MA
3. CCI goes to <100	3. CCI goes to >100
4. Low touch 20 MA and goes below the 20 MA	4. High touch 20 MA or goes above 20 MA
5. Close above 40 MA	5. Close below 40 MA
6. Buy 1 bid above prior day high	6. Sell 1 bid below prior day low
7. Sell to close 1 bid below prior day low	7. Buy to close 1 bid above prior day high

Table 5-1: Summary for Swing Trading Setup

Key Chart Patterns to Note

I would like to share with you some key chart patterns that would be most useful to you in using my swing strategy.

- Measured Pullback

    The pullback must be regular and controlled with small candles (Figure 5-14).

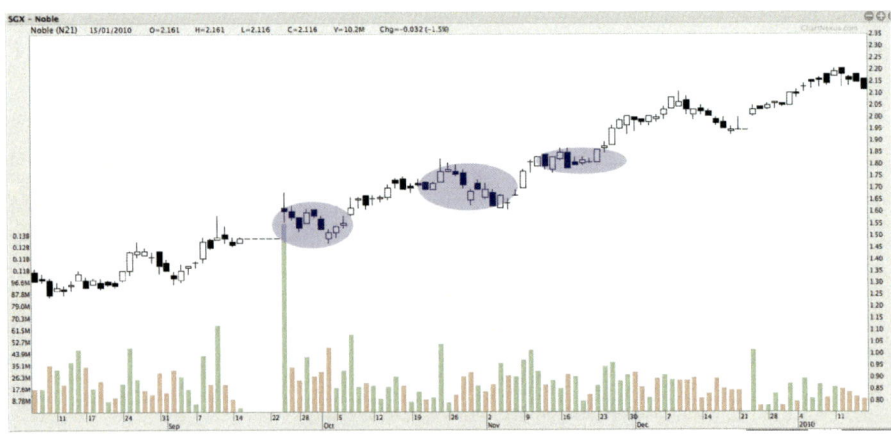

Figure 5-14: Example of measured pullbacks

When you observe a big tank as pullback (Figure 5-15), it is best to give this potential entry a miss. Such volatile price action likely indicates a change in a trend.

Figure 5-15: Example of a big tank as pullback

- Strong Trend With Higher Highs or Lower Lows
  This swing strategy adopts "The Trend Is Your Friend" methodology. Hence, it is important that the trend identified is strong before making an entry decision. In a bullish trend, ensure that the price hits higher highs or, for a bearish trend, lower lows Figures 5-16 and 5-17 are good examples of these.

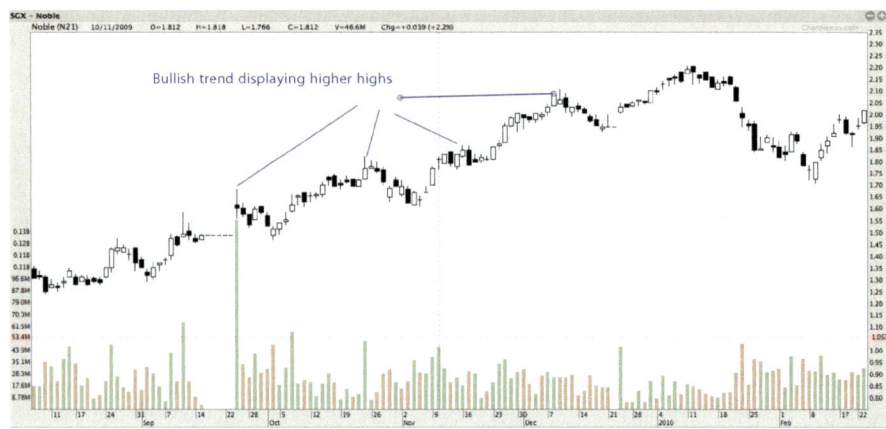

Figure 5-16: A strong bullish trend making higher highs

Figure 5-17: A strong bearish trend making lower lows

Figure 5-18 depicts an unclear trend and entering trades like this will get you nowhere. I advise you to stay away from making any trade until a clear trend is developed. Do not be too eager to enter a trade and keep looking for "creative" opportunities to make a trade, which is a common mistake most amateur traders make. Remember a bullish trend has higher highs and higher lows while a bearish trend has lower lows and lower highs.

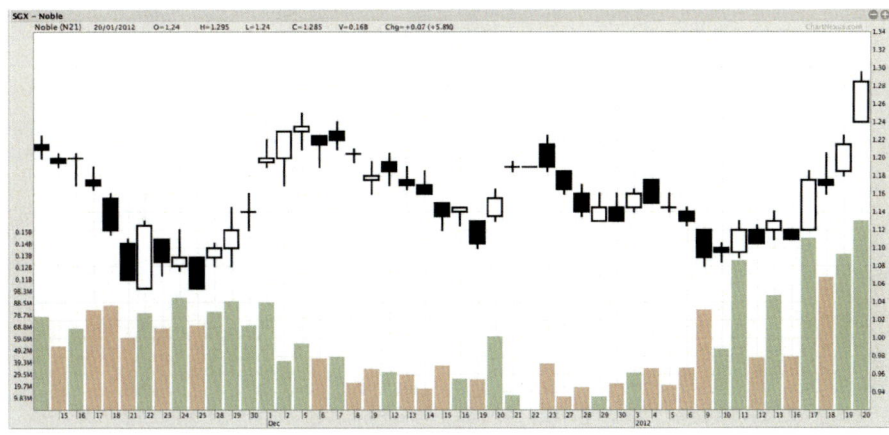

Figure 5-18: Price in consolidation

- Parabolic Movement

  Price should progress gradually and steadily to be qualified as a good potential entry (Figure 5-19).

Figure 5-19a: Price trending gradually and steadily

Figure 5-19b: Price trending gradually and steadily

Beware when you see price moving in a parabolic manner (Figure 5-20). Such drastic movement will most likely result in large "aftershocks" with high volatility. Some may view this profitable, but it is definitely not my cup of tea.

Figure 5-20: Price moving in parabolic manner

Exit Strategy for Swing Trade

Once I made an entry, my first profit target will be at the previous high (for bullish trades). I will take progressive profits when the price hits my first target (Figure 5-21).

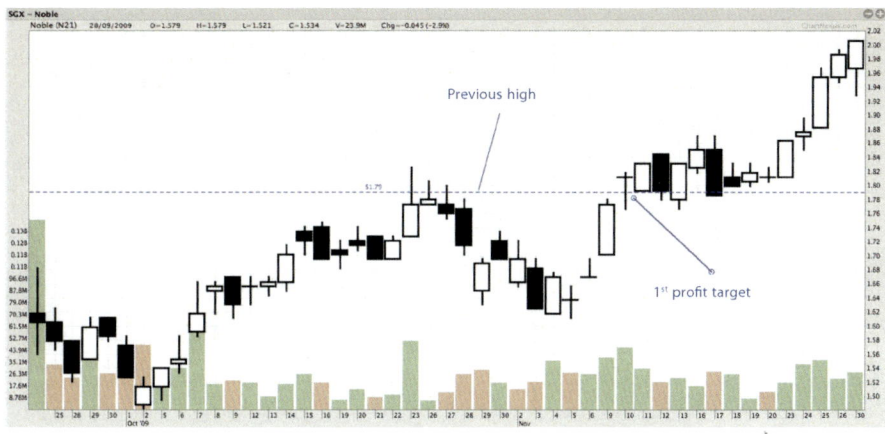

Figure 5-21: Profit taking when prices hit previous high

For this strategy, I will enter all positions (according to my risk management rules) once the buy signal is given. More on Position Sizing will be shared in Chapter 7. For exiting, I will do so by scaling out. This means if the price reaches the previous high or 1 bid below previous high, I will take 30% off the table.

Next, I will study candlestick patterns and will exit another 30% if a doji (which represents a possible trend reverse), bearish engulfing, or any bearish reversal candlestick pattern appears. Lastly, I will exit all positions if the price closes below the low of a doji, which may signify a change in trend direction. The reverse applies for bearish trades (Figure 5-22).

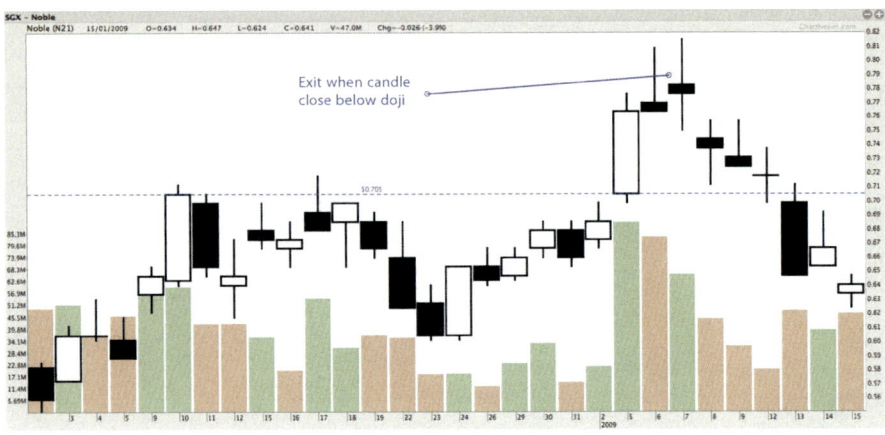

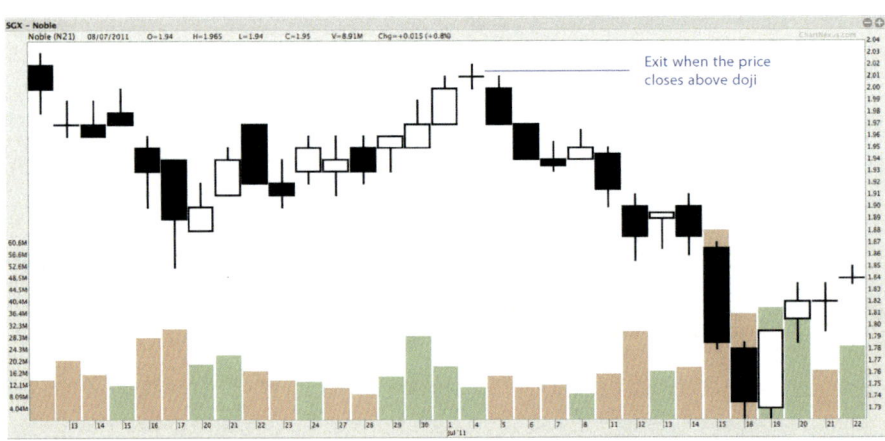

Figure 5-22: Exits using candlestick patterns

Figure 5-23 shows some reliable candlestick patterns which I use to scale out or close a trade.

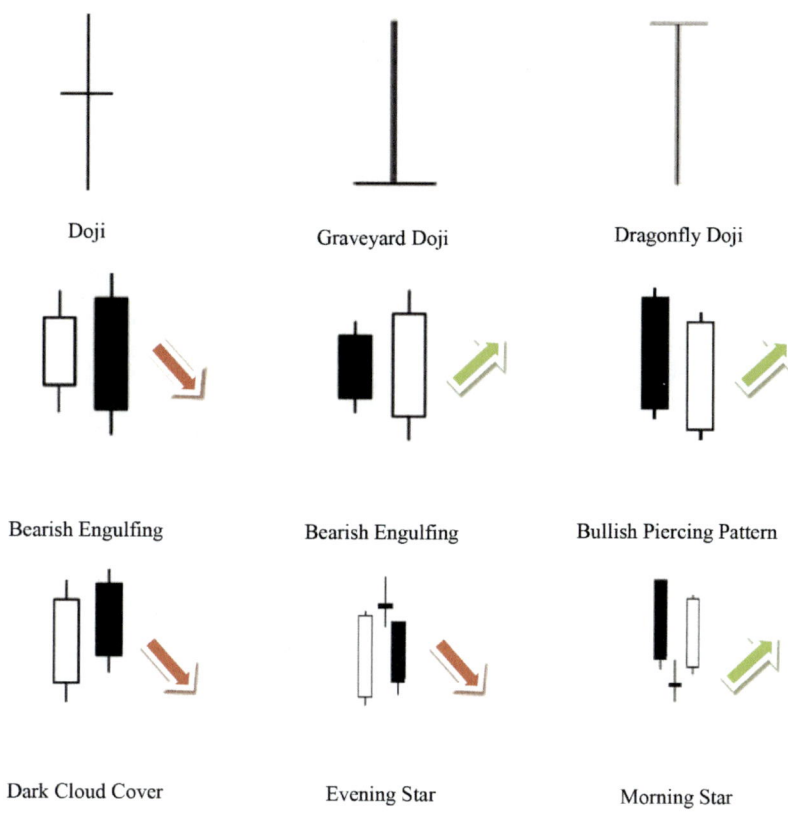

Figure 5-23: Examples of candlestick patterns

Many times in the equity market, price closes above previous swing high or below previous swing low. This is commonly called a "breakout" (Figure 5-24).

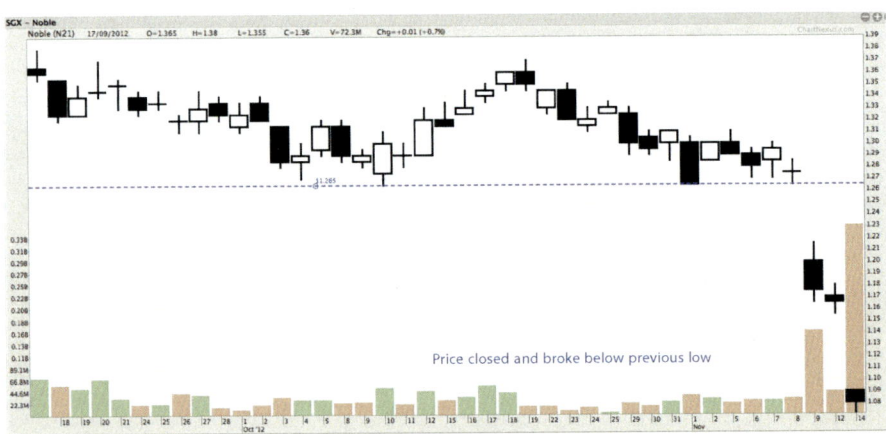

Figure 5-24: Examples of breakouts

Many traders scanning for stocks will generally think that Figure 5-25 shows a good chance to trade a breakout strategy. This means they look for a price that hits higher than the previous swing high, and believe that it will continue higher. Once the market opens the next day, a bullish trade entry will be made. Nevertheless, such price movements frequently call for a false breakout and start to reverse. As such, it is a good time for me to exit for profits (when the price is at or near previous swing high) as I have already entered much earlier (according to my swing strategy) and am already in profit.

In general, this swing trade strategy that I use is for trade retracement, not breakout. Nevertheless, I do not mean that the breakout strategy does not work. You can still make a neat profit if the price goes your way after a breakout. But my experience is that the Probability of Win with a breakout strategy is very low. Many traders choose to give up after suffering a couple of losses. I would rather adopt a strategy with a higher Probability of Win.

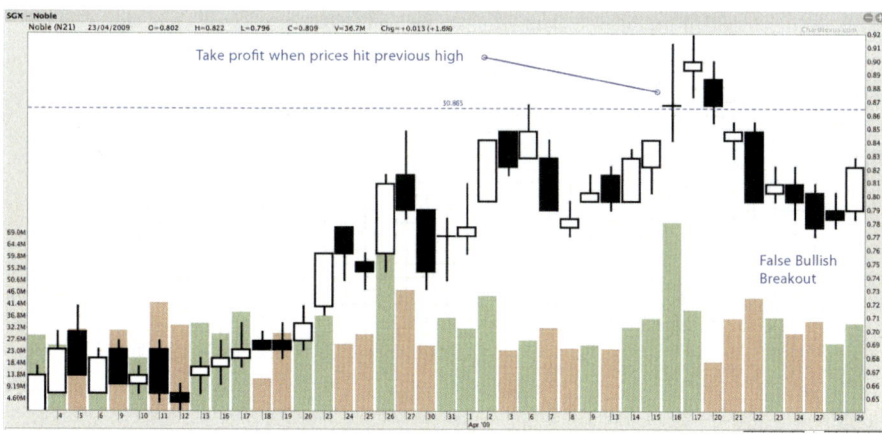

Figure 5-25a: Examples of false breakout

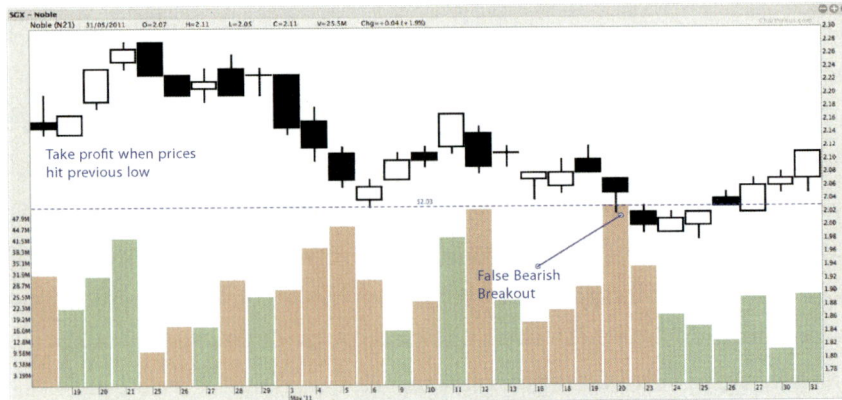

Figure 5-25b: Examples of false breakout

Every time when the price gaps up significantly, it is a good idea to lock in profits as well. How significant it is depends on the stock's history as it is relative to its past data. As a trader, it is important that we also study the pattern and movement of the stock we are trading. Understand its behaviour so that we will not be taken by surprise. For example, if today is the fourth day of my trade and stock price gaps up by, say 2%, I will take partial profits. If price gaps up and reverses to the previous day high, I will also scale out of position (Figure 5-26).

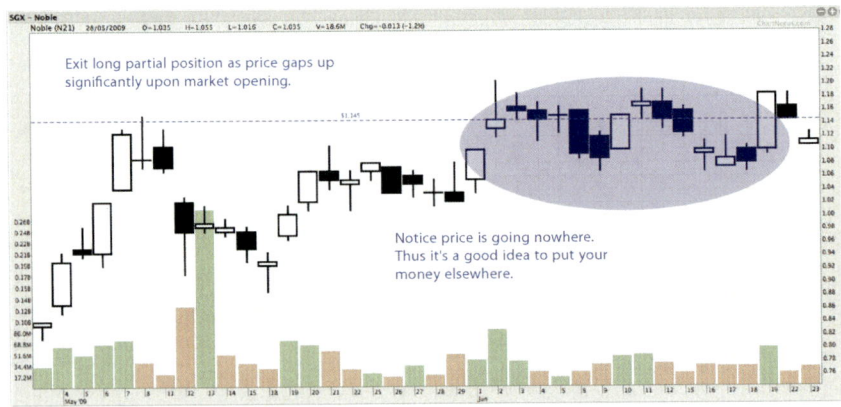

Figure 5-26: Profit take after a gap up

THE KEY IDEA IS TO SCALE OUT OF POSITION PROGRESSIVELY

My time frame for swing trades is five days. This means that I will exit all positions within five days regardless of the price. This is what I call "**Time Stop**". According to experience, if the price do not reach my profit targets within five trading days, it most likely is not going anywhere (Figure 5-27). Under such conditions, I will drop the stock (regardless of whether I am in profit or loss) and use the capital for other opportunities. Do not waste your time and money on a stock that does not make money for you. Exit gracefully as suggested by Time Stop, and carry on your trading journey rather than keep on hoping.

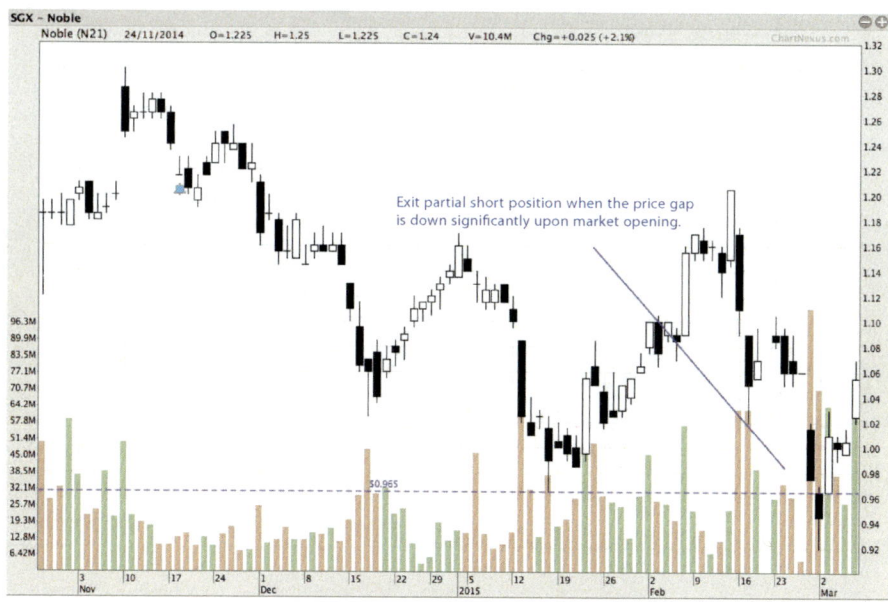

Figure 5-27: Profit take after a gap down

Figure 5-28 shows more examples of my swing trade setups.

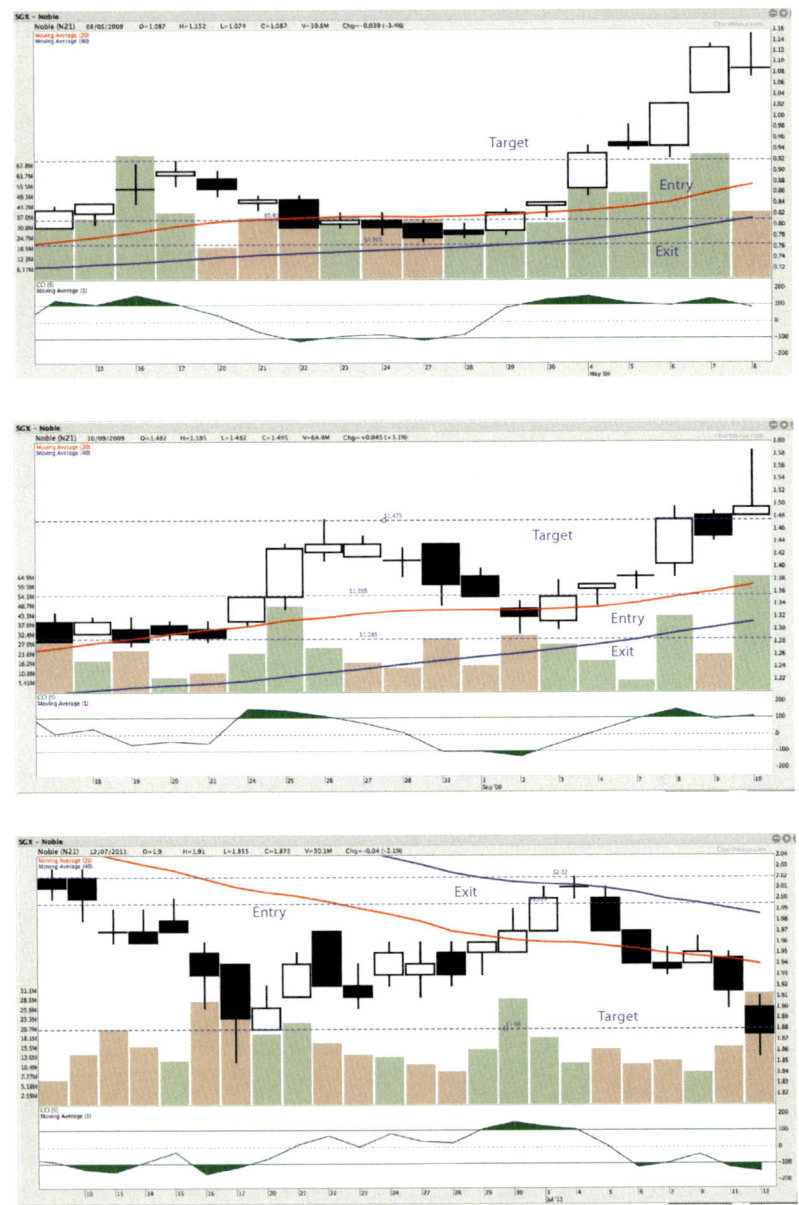

Figure 5-28: Examples of swing trade setups

Importance of Stop-loss

Stop-loss is a very important element in trading. Although important, it is frequently ignored (on purpose) by many traders. The reason why many ignore the need for a stop-loss is because they refuse to admit that their trades have gone wrong. They would rather hope that the price will get back in their favour and turn a loser into a winner. You may be lucky once or twice, but in a long run you will suffer for being so "optimistic".

You cannot be successful in trading by hoping or turning a swing trade into a long-term investment. In my opinion, you cannot gain success in trading unless you are able to embrace the importance of setting a stop-loss in every trade you make. Many traders have learnt this the hard way. Do you want to be one of them?

Now using Figure 5-29, I will share with you how I set my stop-loss every time I make a swing trade.

- 1st stop-loss – initial stop-loss

  Upon entering a trade, the stop-loss is immediately set at the previous day's candle low for bullish trades or the previous day's candle high for bearish trades.

- 2nd stop-loss – break-even stop

  If the price moves up (for bullish trades) or down (for bearish trades) by about 5% in your favour, shift stop-loss to break-even, i.e., at entry price.

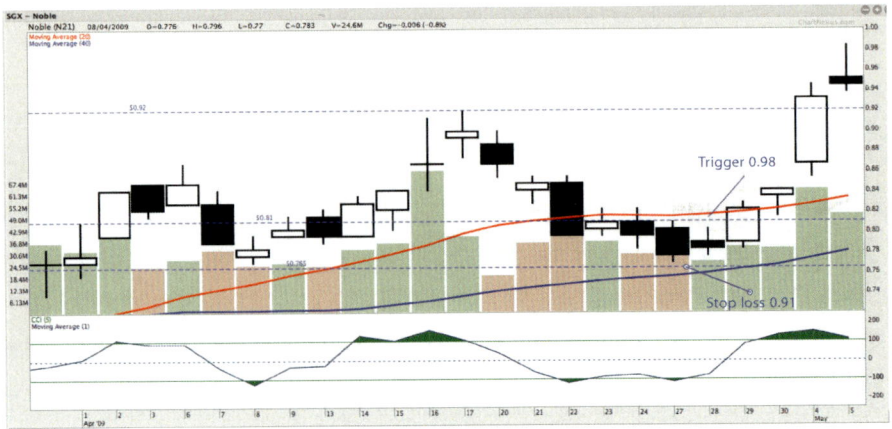

Figure 5-29: Determining stop-loss upon entry

- **3rd stop-loss – trailing stop**
  When the price moves more than 5% in your favour, set your stop-loss to the previous candle low (for bullish trades) or previous candle high (for bearish trades). This will act as an insurance to protect your profits.

- **4th stop-loss – time stop**
  Close all positions after five trading days (excluding entry day), even if the price has yet to hit our target or stop-loss. Also, many would be doing contra and have to buy and sell within five days, so as to profit from the contra gain.

Can you see how structured my stop-loss is? How it is fused seamlessly into my swing trading strategy? For whatever strategy you are using, always have a stop-loss plan in place before making a trade! More often than not, traders decide to cut loss only when the amount lost is too much for them to bear. Do get your trading psychology right before making any trades.

Position Trading Strategy

For my position trading strategy, I would be in a trade for two weeks or longer. I trade the weekly charts for position trading, which is a good strategy for traders who are not able to monitor the market daily. I use two different strategies for position trading, which I will share now.

Cross-over Strategy

For this strategy, I will use 10 EMA and 50 EMA to trade the crossover (see Figure 5-30). Such crossover trades are pretty reliable on weekly charts and they are easy to implement.

Enter a bullish trade once 10 EMA cross above 50 EMA.

Enter a bearish trade once 10 EMA cross below 50 EMA.

Figure 5-30a: Examples of crossover strategy

Figure 5-30b: Examples of crossover strategy

K39 Strategy

K39 is also commonly known as Stochastic 39. As the name suggests, we use the Slow Stochastic indicator with the K parameter set as 39. We do not need the signal line for this strategy.

The setup would be done on the weekly chart as follows:
- Look for K39 line to be above 50 for bullish trade or below 50 for bearish trade.
- Price must trade above previous candle high for bullish trade or below previous candle low for bearish trade.

Looking at Figure 5-31, we can get ready to enter a bearish trade when Stochastic 39 crosses below 50 mark. Execute the trade when the price trades below the previous candle low. The same explanation applies to the chart in Figure 5-32.

Figure 5-31: Examples of K39 strategy

Figure 5-32: Examples of K39 strategy

Which Strategy to Use

I always have traders ask me which strategies are best, which time frame is the best and if there are sure-win strategies that could make an abundance of income without much hard work.

There are no sure-win strategies, what many call "holy grails". No matter how good a strategy is, there are bound to be losing trades, if not losing streaks. I have seen too many traders give up a sound strategy after encountering two to three losses. When a new strategy is adopted, they change strategy again after some losses. This goes on over and over again until either the trading account is empty, or they just get too disappointed.

To me, a strategy is good when Probability of Win is more than 0.5 and Payoff Ratio is more than 1. There will be losing trades along the way, but it is a no brainer that your trading account will grow consistently in a long run. The next question that arises is how a trader knows if the strategy used has a good Probability of Win and Payoff Ratio. This is where extensive back-testing is required and traders need to be diligent in doing so. If you want to be successful in trading, you have to put in the effort and hard work. There is no such thing as easy money. Be wary of empty promises!

Learning Points

- Trading is like an art, not science. Do not be too caught up in looking for the ideal setup.

- The trend is your friend.

- Follow your trading plans and do not anticipate trades.

- When it comes to trading, know your time frame.

- There are four different types of stop-loss: initial, break-even, trailing, and time stop.

- Always know your stop-loss before making a trade.

- Move your stop to break-even when you start to make money.

- Do not give up too soon as success is just around the corner.

Exercise

- What is your ideal Payoff Ratio requirement to enter a trade?

_____

_____

_____

_____

- What should your minimum Probability of Win be for the strategy you are adopting?

_____

_____

_____

_____

- What is/are your stop-loss plan(s)? Please detail your step-by-step plan.

_____

_____

_____

_____

6 | NR7 (NARROW RANGE) & NR4 + ID SHORT-TERM STRATEGIES

I n this chapter, I am going to share with you more strategies that you will find useful and suitable for your trading style. As discussed previously, I am not going to share a strategy and have you adopt it without understanding why and how it works. Hence, I will explain NR7 & NR4 + ID in more detail in this chapter.

In general, there are three basic ways to trade the market. They are trading retracement, trading breakouts, and trading volatility.

Trading Retracement

Figure 6-1 shows the price in a bullish trend. As we think the bullish trend will persist, you will look to long, thus buying at a dip.

Figure 6-1: Price retracing in a bullish trend

Trading Breakout

In Figure 6-2, you enter when the price breaks and closes above the previous high. Such a strategy may give you lucrative returns if the breakout is sustainable. Many traders give up this strategy as they may encounter many false breakouts. Can you imagine the outcome with many false breakouts coupled with poor money management? A lot of determination and discipline is required to adopt this strategy religiously. Traders adopting this strategy must have the commitment to cut loss when the breakout is a false one.

Figure 6-2: Price breaking out

Trading Volatility

Now, I am going to share with you Narrow Range (NR) trading, which is most efficient for trading volatility (Figure 6-3). Created by Toby Crabel, the NR strategy can be used for counter-trend trades. NR trades are usually short-term trades and it takes **two to three days** to open and close a trade.

Figure 6-3: Price with high volatility

The thinking behind the pattern is that price volatility acts like a spring being wound. It is under pressure, ever waiting to be released. The direction of the release cannot be accurately predicted, but the move is sometimes a violent one.

Hint: **The shorter the height (length of candle), the tighter the spring and hence, the bigger the move!**

THE MARKET GOES THROUGH CONTINUAL CYCLES OF INTENSE ACTIVITY FOLLOWED BY PERIODS OF RELATIVE CALM

Narrow Range (NR) 7

For NR7 trades, we are looking for the narrowest or smallest candle range (including tail of candle) in the last seven days. Such phenomenon represents a pause in the market, waiting for a big move to happen. Remember the "spring" analogy I used earlier? This is the volatility we look and wait for.

Instead of staring at the charts and counting the candles, you can simply use ChartNexus to scan all the stocks that will present results that satisfy NR7 criteria. In Figure 6-4, the candles indicated by an arrow represent the narrowest range candle in the last seven days.

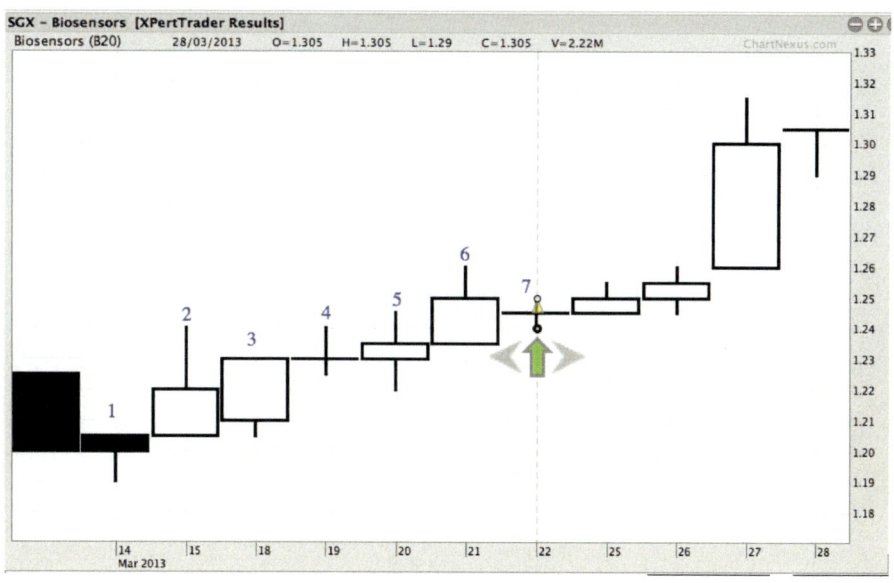

Figure 6-4a: Examples of NR7 trade

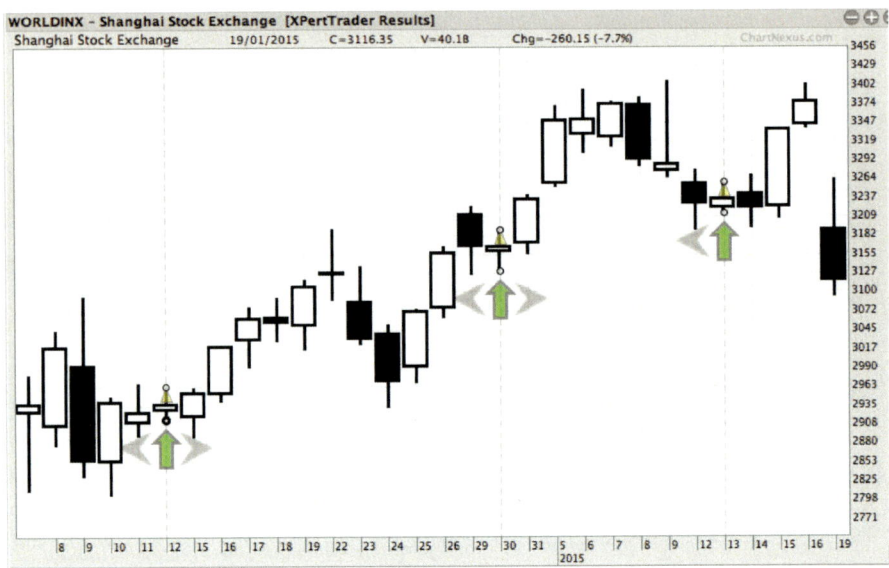

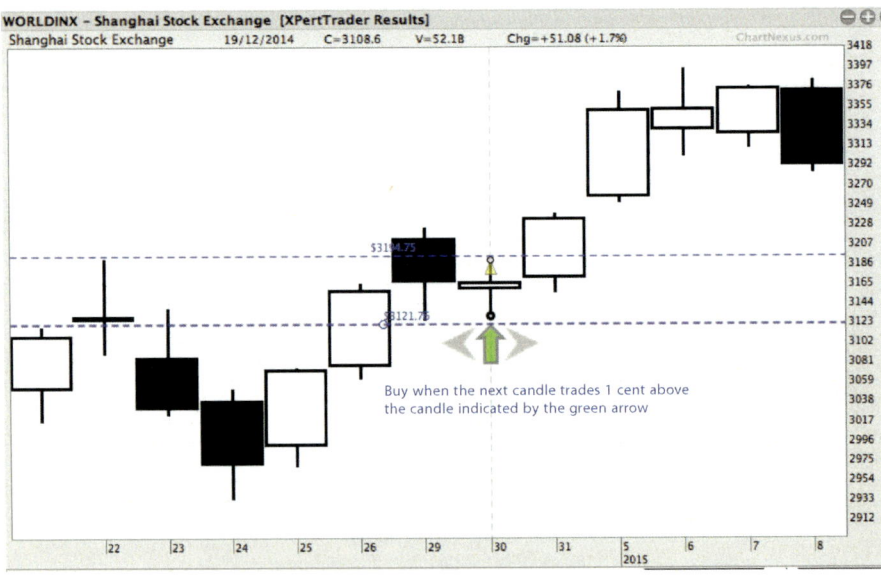

Figure 6-4b: Examples of NR7 trade

When an arrow is spotted, place an order to buy if the next or following candles trades 1 cent above the high of the candle indicated by the arrow, or sell if the next or following candles trades 1 cent below the low of the candle indicated by the arrow. Whichever order triggers, cancel the other order and replace it with a stop-loss order. The stop-loss can be placed 1 cent below the low of the candle indicated by the arrow if it is a long trade.

Narrow Range (NR) 4

NR4 must be combined with Inside Day (ID), what many call "harami" in candlestick patterns. You can see some examples of harami in Figure 6-5.

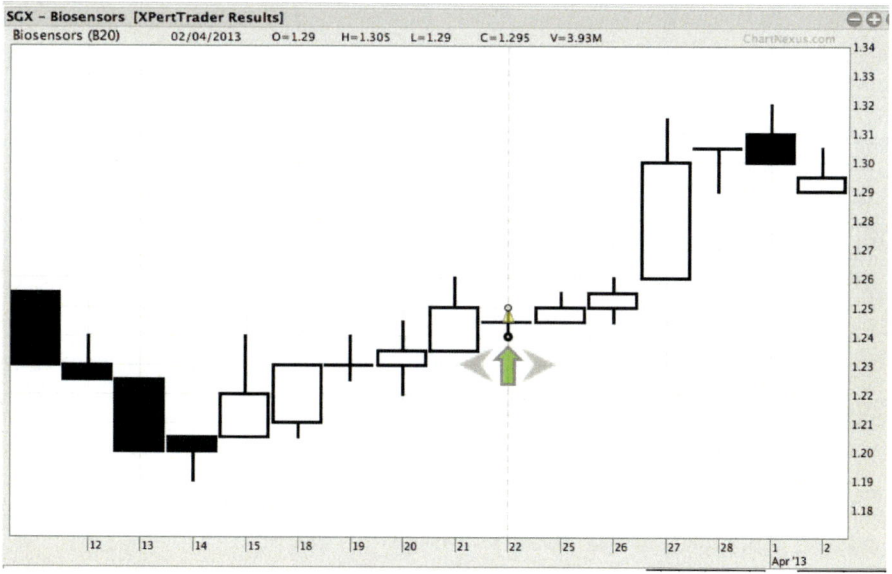

Figure 6-5: Examples of harami

Generally, for NR4 + ID trades, we look for the narrowest or smallest candle (including tail of candle) of the last four days' candles, together with a harami pattern (Figure 6-6). This is represented by green arrows in our examples and it can be programmed in the ChartNexus platform.

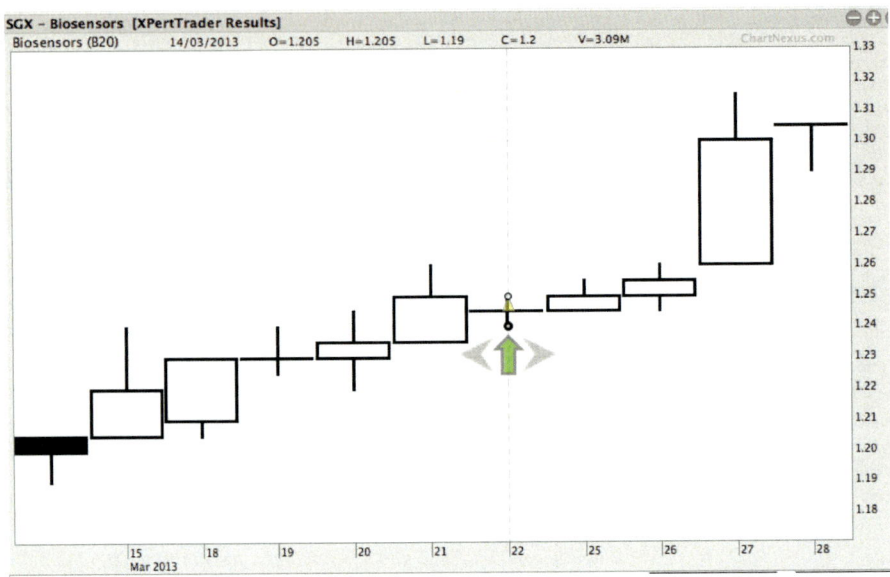

Figure 6-6: Examples of NR4 trade

When an arrow is spotted, place an order to buy if the next or following candles trades 1 cent above the high of candle indicated by the arrow, or sell if the next or following candles trades 1 cent below the low of the candle indicated by the arrow. Whichever order triggers, cancel the other order and replace it with a stop-loss order. The stop-loss can be placed 1 cent below the low of candle indicated by the arrow if it is a long trade or 1 cent above the candle indicated by the arrow if it is a short trade.

One of the reasons why traders like this strategy is because the loss/
risk is very small, while the profit target/reward can be very big, hence
delivering a high Payoff Ratio. The underlying principle is that the
market goes through periods of quiet and periods of volatility. When it
is quiet, we foresee a big move later. Perhaps this is what is known as
the "calm before the storm".

Although the Probability of Win for NR strategy alone is about 0.5, you
can increase it by combining technical analysis studies such as support,
resistance, Fibonacci, etc. In Figure 6-7, you can see there is a lot of
sideways movement or prolonged consolidation. When a NR appears,
you see there is a strong support, which will likely limit your profit
potential if entering a short trade. Under such situations, you may wish
to give this trade a miss, as your profits may be limited. Always keep
Payoff Ratio in mind before making any trades. We do not want many
small wins but your trading account jeopardised due to one big loss.

Figure 6-7: Example of NR trade coupled with technical analysis

Although you can increase your probability of win, do not fall into the trap of having too many technical analysis or indicators in your charts. I know many traders fall into this trap. They can wait forever, looking for a chance to get into a trade. How much is enough? I believe this is a frequently asked question. Honestly, I have no "one size fits all" answer to that. It all based on your experience, your understanding of the strategy adopted and your knowledge of the market you are trading. That is also why I keep stressing the need to understand the strategy you are using and to back-test it diligently. If you have so many indicators and lines on your charts that you are not able to see your candles, this may be a sign for you to reduce what you have.

Profit Taking

Profit taking techniques for NR4 and NR7 trades is similar to that of the swing trade, which I introduced earlier. For this strategy, always look into taking progressive profits. You can also profit take by reading candlestick patterns. The candlestick pattern is a simple yet powerful tool used in trading.

An important note is that the NR trade is an intra-day or a multi day strategy. You only have one chance to get it wrong. For example, say a bullish NR trade setup appears and you make a bullish trade. Within the same day, if it goes south and hits your pre-defined stop-loss while initiating a sell, you can still execute a short trade. But if the price next goes north again hitting your stop-loss and initiating a buy, you cannot make any more trades for the day. Nevertheless, as shared earlier, you can use support and resistance (or other technical analysis) to filter trades with low Payoff Ratio, because this is a sign that the market is still in consolidation.

Conclusion

This strategy is suitable for traders who wish to trade short term. Like any other strategy, traders have to ensure a Probability of Win of more than 0.5 and a Payoff Ratio of more than 1 in order to be profitable in the long run. Traders adapting this strategy must follow strict money management rules and have the discipline to adhere closely to it!

I summarise the setup for NR7 and NR4+ID this way:

Set up: Place an order to buy a cent above the high, or short a cent below the low of the candle indicated by the arrow.

Trigger: Whichever order triggers, cancel the other order and replace it with a stop-loss order. Ride price following the new trend until the swing ends.

Profit Take: Take profits based on candlestick patterns.

Learning Points

- The market goes through different periods: peaceful and quiet, or violent and noisy.

- Volume first, followed by price.

- The more peaceful the market is now, the more violent its next move will be.

- The key to NR trade is a tight stop-loss and a potentially large profit.

Exercise

- Using the NR7 & NR4+ID strategy, identify the entries and exits using the following charts in Figure 6-8.

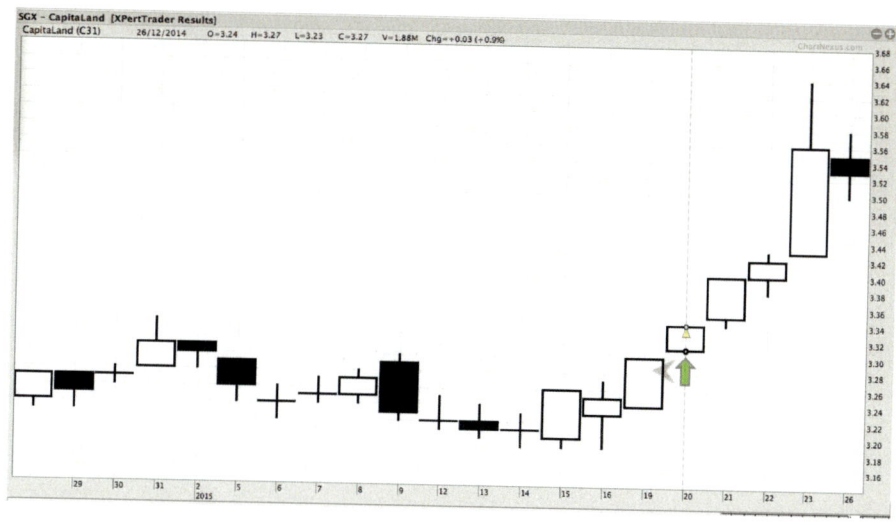

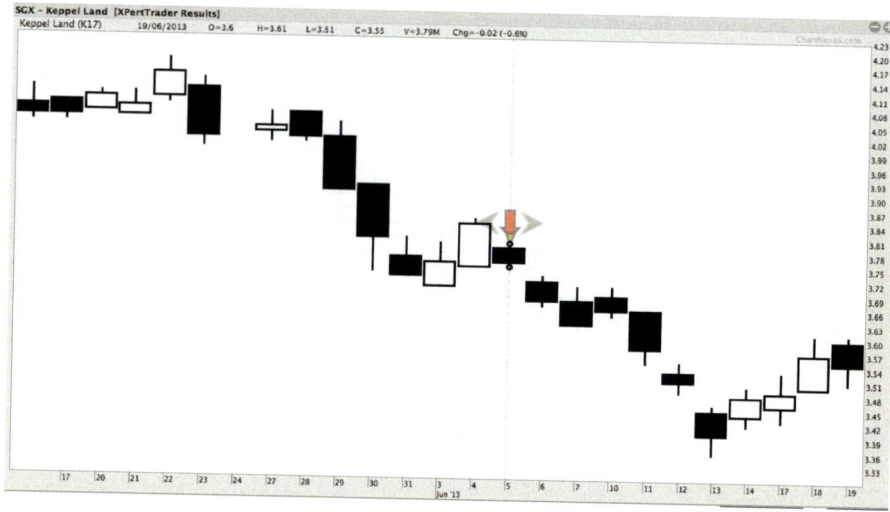

Figure 6-8: Identifying entries and exits

Part II

FIGHTING THE INNER WAR

"Know your enemy and know yourself and you can fight a hundred battles without disaster."
– Sun Tzu

To win a war, not only do you need to know your enemy, you also need to know yourself very well. This is a critical factor for every successful trader.

Plan your trades and trade your plans. To do this effectively, you need to take charge of your own psychology. Do not let the market take control of it.

7 | THE IMPORTANCE OF POSITION SIZING

I cannot stress enough the importance of Position Sizing when it comes to trading. It is why this chapter is dedicated to position sizing.

> **NOT PRACTISING A HABIT OF GOOD POSITION SIZING IS A SURE WAY TO FAIL IN TRADING**

Many traders burst their account because of over-trading (a badly sized trade), where they put in too much money in a single trade that turns out to be wrong. They could have had many winning trades before, but one single oversized trade that goes wrong can ruin your trading account. Too small a sizing does not work either as it takes you longer than it should to reach your trading objectives. This frustrates many traders. Eventually, they give up trading.

You would have known by now that I have strategies for short and long term trading (swing and position trading respectively). Let's do a quick recap: my short term strategies are Swing Trades and NR Trades, while my longer term strategy is the TradersGPS. As far as position sizing is concerned, I have different approaches for short and long term trades. In trading, you seldom find a "one size fits all" technique or strategy. It is important for you to understand the grounds of what you are doing. Do not be too eager to embark on the action of trading and forgo the learning process.

For *long-term position sizing*, we aim to accumulate or build up positions for a stock over time, thus creating a pyramid pattern (Figure 7-1).

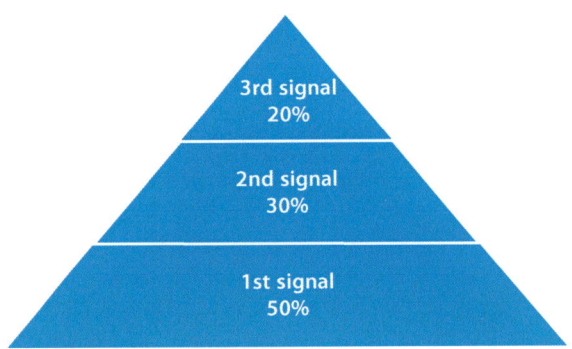

Figure 7-1: Pyramid pattern for long-term position sizing

You want to buy more positions upon the first entry signal and fewer positions upon subsequent re-enter signals. This simply means that the position to add-on (for a single counter/stock) gets smaller as the trend progresses or matures (Figure 7-2).

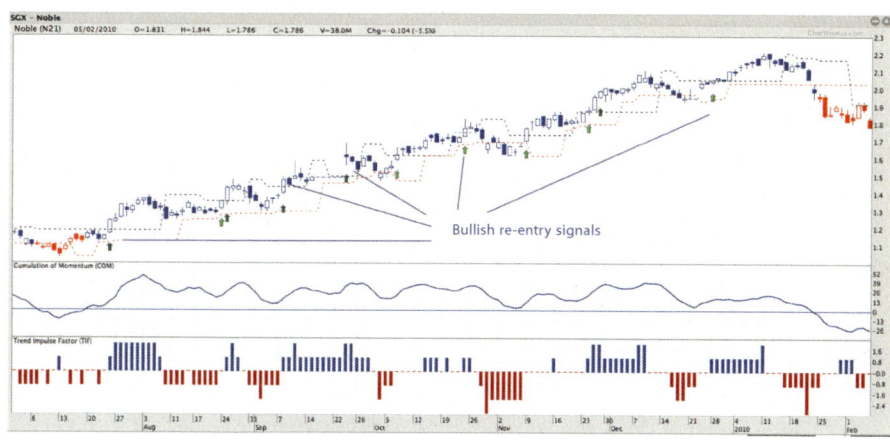

Figure 7-2: Adding on to winning positions

Once you have committed 100% for a stock, you should be in the money already. 100% committed means the total allowable amount has been allocated for that particular trade, based on your position sizing rule. You may also wish to keep adding 10% for every re-entry signal until the signal to exit appears, i.e. colour of the candlestick changes or when the price breaks trough (for long position) or peaks (for short position) in the TradersGPS. Under such conditions where the exit signal appears, close all positions you have for that stock.

BUY MORE WHEN I AM RIGHT, BE DECISIVE AND SELL FAST WHEN I AM WRONG

That is my secret to success in trading. Are you willing to do the same?

Many ask, why not enter 100% when the entry signal appears? My explanation is that when a trend is beginning, it has not yet matured.

The probability of a wrong signal is high. An entry technique of scaling in minimises your losses in the case that you are wrong. We add on fewer positions as the trend progresses as it may be near the maturing stage. Further upside potential may be limited. We have to face the fact that there will be losing trades no matter how powerful your strategy is. In trading, we must always strive to minimise losses and ride on the gains. Adding on to position when you are right allows you to take full advantage of the ride.

SCALE IN WHEN YOU ARE RIGHT. YOUR LOSSES WILL BE SMALL IF YOU ARE WRONG

For short-term position sizing, I am only willing to risk 2% of my trading capital for every trade made. For swing trades (short-term trading), we enter 100% upon entry signal and exit progressively upon every exit signal.

I believe the question in your mind now will be what trading capital am I talking about. To answer that, we need to talk about the Position Sizing Plan (PSP). In PSP, we split our money allocated for trading into two parts, one for short-term trading while the other for long-term trading (Figure 7-3).

For example, if you set aside $100,000 for trading, you may allocate 70% of the money for long-term trading and the remainder 30% for short-term trading. So now you have $70,000 and $30,000 for long and short term trading respectively.

TRADE SHORT TERM FOR INCOME; TRADE LONG TERM FOR WEALTH ACCUMULATION

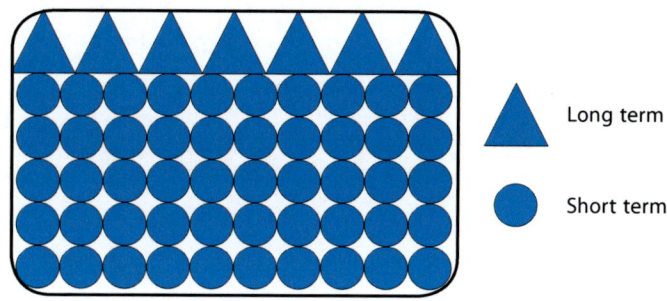

Figure 7-3: Money allocation

With $70,000 for long-term trading, say you want to trade seven different stocks in your watch-list, $10,000 have to be set aside for each stock, waiting for opportunities to arise. Look at Figure 7-4. When entry signals are given for each stock, we enter accumulatively according to plan, i.e. 50% ($5,000 for this example) for 1st entry signal, 30% for 2nd re-entry signal, and 20% for 3rd re-entry signal.

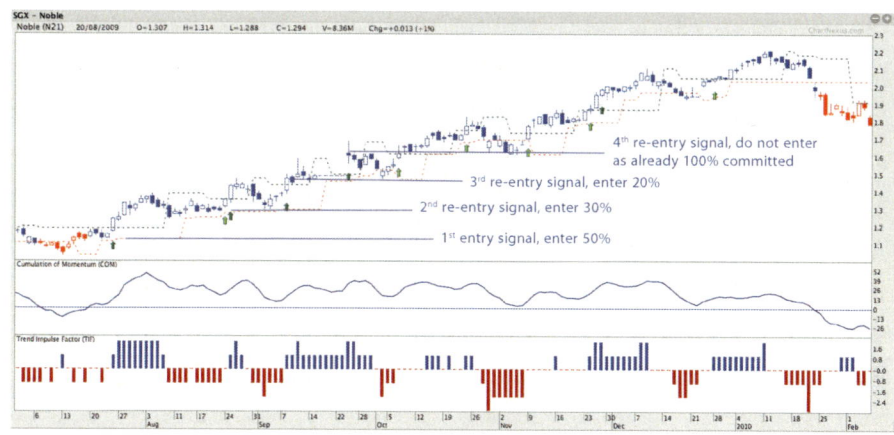

Figure 7-4: Adding on to winning positions

With this technique, you may not be 100% invested (for a stock), but once you are 100% invested (in this example, you have already bought or sold $10,000 worth of shares), you should already be profitable. You are simply waiting for an exit signal to take profit. Using a systematic rule-based approach to entries and exits helps remove the emotional decision-making component from the trader.

As mentioned earlier, I adopt a different plan for short-term position sizing. With the $30,000 set aside for short-term trading, I am willing to risk 2% of the $30,000 for every trade. That means I lose only $600 if a trade goes wrong. The 2% mean you are "splitting" this $30,000 into 50 tokens. Each time you make a trade, one token is used. Every time you put in one token, there are two elements you should be most concerned with: Payoff Ratio and Probability of Win. Generally, you want a Payoff Ratio of more than 1 and a Probability of Win more than 0.5 in order to stay profitable in the long run. Under such criteria, it is a mere matter of time before making money from trading.

Next for short-term trading, we have to know how to calculate the quantity to buy for a stock so that your loss is always limited to $600 per trade. To work out the quantity, you need to pre-determine your stop-loss price. Many traders enter a trade without first defining the stop-loss region or price. Some traders even do not know that there is a need for stop-loss! Do note that without a stop-loss, it is like taking a roller coaster ride without a safety belt. If you do not fall, you would have gained thrill and excitement. But if you do fall, that would be the last thing you do in life! The same applies to trading. One bad trade may be your last trade if not managed properly.

For example, your entry price is $1.20 and you identify your stop-loss to be at $1.15.

Shares to buy = 600/ (1.20 − 1.15) = 12,000 shares (12 lots)

Thus, you would be spending $1.20 x 12,000 = $14,400 to make this trade. Your loss would be limited to $600 should the trade go wrong.

The secret to succeed in trading is to be able to repeat this process over and over again without fail. It is that simple! Do not deviate or keep searching high and low for another "sure win" strategy that offers no losing trade. Use that energy to focus on following your trade rules and doing up your trading journal instead. Trust me, you would be much better off this way.

By now, you would probably know that there are different permutations of right and wrong trades. This is regardless of the strategy you are using, the market you are trading and which time frame you are in.

Out of 10 trades, your permutation could be:

Lose, Win, Win, Lose, Win, Win, Win, Lose, Win, Lose

It could also be:

Win, Lose, Lose, Lose, Lose, Win, Win, Win, Win, Win

If you have poor money management strategy with this latter permutation, there is a high chance that your trading account would be wiped out before you can enjoy the series of wins right after the string of losses. From experience, having a string of losing streaks is pretty common in trading. The only way to get over this is to adopt good money management rules, coupled with good Payoff Ratio and Probability of Win.

With a 2% risk, the Payoff Ratio of more than 1 and a sound strategy offering Probability of Win of more than 0.5, it is almost impossible to get 50 consecutive losing trades where your account get wiped out completely.

It is extremely important to strictly follow your own trading and money management rules. Both must take place in order to be successful in trading in the long run. You must learn to cut loss when needed to so as to remain in this game. Failing to do so may cause your trading capital to suffer a bigger than expected drawdown.

IN TRADING, YOU DO NOT HOPE, PRAY OR PROCRASTINATE. YOU SIMPLY FOLLOW THE RULES

You can have a better idea of what I mean by looking at Table 7-1. If you cut loss too late and suffer a 5% drawdown from your trading capital, you need a 5.3% gain to recover what you had lost. If you refuse to cut loss as per your rules, and at last decided to so while suffering a 50% drawdown, you need to make a 100% gain in order to break-even! By a glance, you know you are playing a losing game if you do not adhere to your own trading rules. What are your purpose and reasons for trading? Focus on trading well instead of making money.

Drawdown	Gain to Recover
2%	2% Gain
5%	5.3% Gain
10%	11.1% Gain
15%	17.6% Gain
20%	25% Gain
25%	33% Gain
30%	42.9% Gain
40%	66.7% Gain
50%	100% Gain
60%	150% Gain
75%	300% Gain
90%	900% Gain

Table 7-1: Managing trading capital

Risk Management

Risk management is a very important component in trading, but conveniently or intentionally ignored by many traders. Most traders do not understand the need for it until their trading account is in a danger zone, after which they regret not obeying their own trading rules and applying good risk management.

Each time before entering a trade, you must already have an idea on how much you are willing to lose. Once a setup appears, check that you have a good Payoff Ratio. With your risk determined, calculate the number of lots you can buy (position sizing) so that the amount of money lost is well within your expectation if the trade turns sour.

YOU ARE OPENING DOORS TO A SUCCESSFUL TRADING WHEN YOU EMBRACE GOOD RISK MANAGEMENT

There are a few different ways to manage trading risk. The following are a few quick concepts for your reference. You can do further research once you identify a method that suits you and your trading goals.

- **Fixed Dollar Risk**

   This is an arbitrary amount that you are prepared to lose should your trade turn sour. This can be any sum comfortable to you. There is no scientific or mathematical way to derive this amount. It is simply based on your comfort level, an amount that would not affect you too much if lost.

   For example, I am willing to lose $500 for every trade should it go bad. A buy signal is given; the current stock price is now $1. Next, I check that the next resistance is at $2. My support, also my stop-loss region, is at $1.50. Under this scenario, my Payoff Ratio is 2 which proves to be attractive to me.

Since my stop-loss is $0.50 away from my entry price and I am comfortable with losing $500 should the trade turn sour, the number of shares I can buy is:

No. of shares = 500/0.5 = 1000

Commission and other fees are excluded in calculation for simplicity.

While it is easy to use, the amount of risk taken in this technique for every trade is based on individual preference, which does not form a firm basis. A trader may have a big risk appetite and is comfortable losing $1,000 for every trade made. If the trader's total trading capital amounts to $5,000, it takes five consecutive losing trades (which is highly possible) to get wiped out. Suppose you spot an entry opportunity that satisfies your strategy criteria. You have to next identify the stop-loss and profit-target region. With that, determine what the Payoff Ratio is, if this trade is worth the risk. In this example in Figure 7-5, the ratio is more than 1—a green light.

The entry price is $1.35 with stop-loss at $1.29

If you decided to lose $1000 for every trade made, hence:

No. of shares =1000/(1.35-1.29) = 16,666 shares

As such, for this trade you can buy 16,666 and risk $1000 in the event the trade turns sour.

Figure 7-5: Example of Fixed Dollar Risk

- **Fixed Percentage Risk**

You determine a percentage in which you are willing or comfortable to lose, should the trade turn against you. You will always be using this percentage number to calculate the number of shares to buy with respect to your trading capital.

Take, for example, you are comfortable with losing 10% of your trading capital for every trade made. For a trading capital of $10,000, 10% is $1,000. As such, $1,000 is the amount you are ready to lose should the trade turn out to be bad. If the trade did turn out to be a losing one, your capital is now $9,000. Your risk is 10% of $9,000, which is $900. As such, your risk amount varies depending on your trading capital.

Personally, I do not apply Fixed Percentage Risk because I think it is tedious to have to calculate the amount to risk for every trade.

Example: Fixed Percentage Risk

For this example, let's assume you have $5,000 as your trading capital and you are only willing to lose 5% for every trade made.

As stated earlier, you have $5,000 as trading capital. 5% is $250.

- **Risk based on ATR**

ATR is the acronym for **Average True Range**. Basically, it is an indicator that measures volatility. Using this risk management technique, the amount of money you may potentially lose in every trade made depends on the volatility at the time of entry.

Every stock behaves differently depending on its volatility. Volatile stocks have bigger swings and movement while less volatile stocks are calm and steady. Even for the same stock, its volatility varies depending on market conditions.

When volatility is high, the number of shares bought can be fewer as your stop-loss will be further away from entry price. This is to ensure that your trade does not get whipsawed unnecessarily due to the big move from stock price. In contrast, you can buy or sell more stocks when the volatility is low as your stop-loss can be nearer to entry price. Low volatility means the move will be smooth and calm without too many "surprise" movements, while keeping your winnings substantial when the price reaches your profit-target region.

Example: Risk based on ATR

For this method, you need to first determine the amount to risk for every trade. For simplicity's sake, let us take this figure to be $1,000.

The stop-loss would be: Entry price − (C x ATR)

C is a constant that typically ranges from 1.5 to 5, depending on your risk appetite. For this example, let us take C = 1.5

In Figure 7-6, the entry setup happens at the vertical dotted line. At that point, ATR reads 0.076

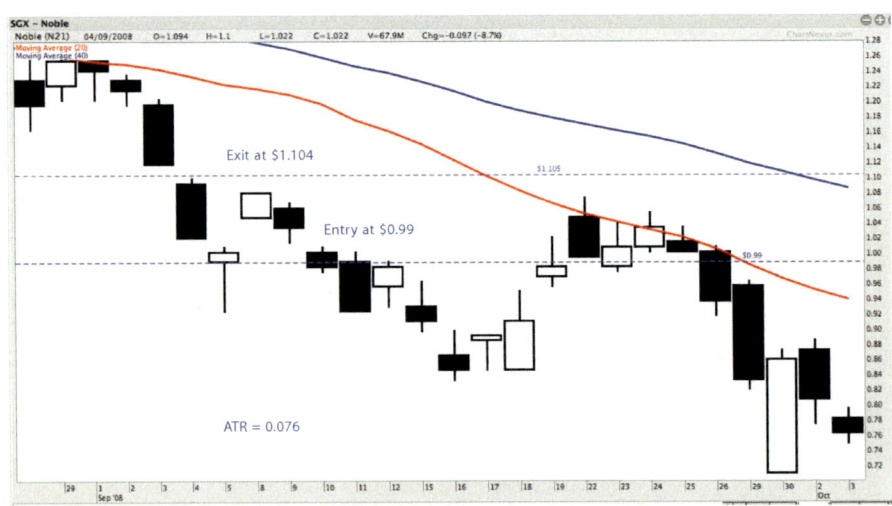

Figure 7-6: Example of Risk based on ATR

The stop-loss is calculated to be: 0.99 + (1.5 x 0.076) = 1.104

For simplicity, let us believe that the Payoff Ratio is more than 1 for this trade. As such, the number of shares to purchase is:

No. of shares = 1000/(1.104-0.99) ~ 8800 shares

In the event this trade turns out to be sour, you lose $1,000 as planned.

When the stock is undergoing a high volatility period, the ATR reading may be higher. With that, your stop-loss price can be much further away from your entry price. This in turn allows the trader to purchase fewer shares so that the risk is still $1,000.

The reverse is true for bearish trades.

Fixed Percentage on Capital

This is what I recommend and have been using. I am willing to risk 2% of my trading capital in every trade made. Say for example, I have $100,000 as my trading capital. 2% is $2,000, which is the amount I am willing to lose for every trade gone badly. This amount of risk remains constant regardless of the size of my trading capital.

From another perspective, with a 2% risk, my entire trading capital will only be wiped out if I suffered 50 consecutive losses. Depending on the Probability of Win of your strategy, you may wish to add on to your fixed percentage, for example, from 2%

to 4%. Due to its simplicity and flexibility, it has always been the technique I adopt religiously.

Example: Fixed Percentage on Capital

For this method, you must first determine the Percentage you are willing or comfortable to lose. It is also important this figure does not cause you a huge drawdown after a few string of losses.

Let me take it as risking 5% of my $10,000 trading capital. This works out to be $500 at risk for every trade made. This would also mean I need twenty consecutive losses to declare bankruptcy. You have to look seriously into your trading strategy if your Probability of Win is that ridiculously low.

Again, for this example, I am willing to lose 5% of my (initial) trading capital amount. Let's say I started trading with an initial capital of $50,000, 5% of which would be $2,500. As such, I am only willing to lose $2,500 for every trade made.

For this trade, the number of shares to short is:

No. of shares = 2500/(1.95-1.83) ~ 20,000 shares

With 20,000 shorted, I lose $2,500 as **planned** should the trade turn sour.

Traders' Risk

Traders should always be aware of the amount of exposure they are taking in the market at all times. Do not risk putting all your money or savings in the market or into a particular stock!

We must trade with money we can afford to lose, without affecting our daily life even if we have lost every single cent to the market. By containing our risk, we can trade with ease of mind and not worry about meals the next month or the one after next. Emotion, the traders' worst enemy, can be minimised this way and you stand a higher chance of attaining success in trading. I urge you to spend time working on your accounts to determine the amount of money to be set aside for trading the market.

Different sectors offer different risks and rewards. Some sectors are more volatile, behaving like wild animals while some are more tame. It is also important for you to understand how the different sectors behave and identify which sectors you should put your money in.

Do not be too ambitious by having all your money in high volatile sectors, hoping to reap more profits in a short period of time. Remember, high returns may invite high risks too. Do your studies carefully. Ensure you practise good money management at all times! You may wish to spread your risk by putting your money into different sectors with different behaviour and volatility.

Learning Points

- When you scale in positions, your losses will be smaller in the case that you are wrong.

- Trade short term for income; trade long term for wealth accumulation.

- Be ready to embrace the success of trading when you open the door of good risk management.

- After buying a stock, new traders think of when they can take profit; before buying a stock, professionals think of where they can put their stop-loss.

- Take care of the stop-loss and the profit will take care of itself.

Exercise

- How much capital would you allocate for long-term trading?

  _____

  _____

  _____

  _____

- How much capital would you allocate for short-term trading?

  _____

  _____

  _____

  _____

- What is your risk management technique and how much are you prepared to lose for every trade made?

  _____

  _____

  _____

  _____

8 PSYCHOLOGY OF TRADING

"If you know your enemies and know yourself, you will not be imperilled in a hundred battles; if you do not know your enemies but do know yourself, you will win one and lose one; if you do not know your enemies nor yourself, you will be imperilled in every single battle."
- Sun Tzu

To be successful and profitable as a trader, you must know yourself and the market. An effective way to do so is with a trading journal. This is a record of all the trades you make and the logic behind all entries and exits. Keeping a trading journal is an important process that you will definitely benefit from, if done properly and diligently.

With a trading journal, you create a "feedback loop" on your trades done (see Figures 8-1 and 8-2). As such, you will know what you did right or wrong after closing a trade. If you made a loss, what went wrong? If you gained a profit, what did you do right and how can you repeat the process? The key word here is "**repeat**". In order to purposefully replicate your successful trades, you must first know what you did right.

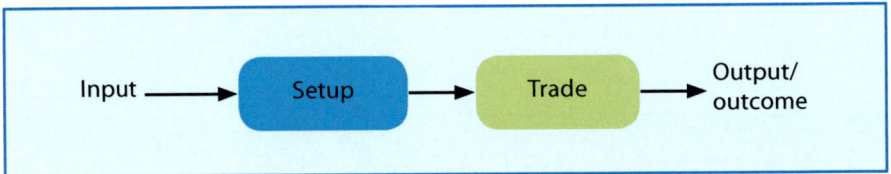

Figure 8-1: A system without a feedback loop

Nevertheless, losing money does not necessarily mean the trade was bad. Remember, there will always be losing trades no matter how good or powerful your strategies are. More importantly, you must know if you had followed your own rules or if you had executed your setups correctly as planned. Many traders beat themselves up for every losing trade they had. As a trader, you must always think in terms of probability; having losing trades is part of the game. Trading is nothing but simply a game of probability.

Having a trading journal is the best way for you as a trader, to constantly keep track of your own performance and learning about yourself. With trading journals, you can fine-tune your trading plans and more importantly, your behaviour when trading. For the losing trades, was your stop-loss too tight? Did you enter too early even before the entry signals were given? Were you too greedy hoping for more, when the signal to take profit was given? With all these questions answered, you can know what went wrong or right with your trades. You can then make the necessary improvements or adjustments to your entries, exits, and even your trading strategy as well as psychology. This will over time, increase your ability to trade better, eventually being profitable

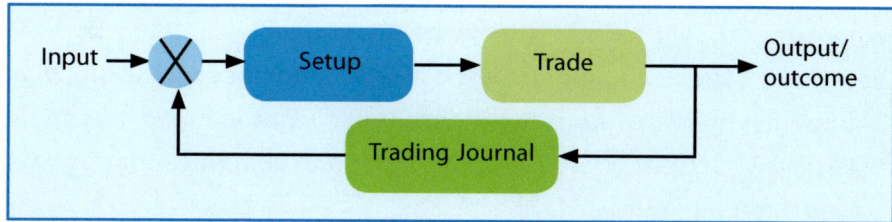

Figure 8-2: A system with trading journal as a feedback loop

consistently! This can only be achieved when you constantly keep records in your trading journal.

What should be recorded in your trading journal?

For me, I record the ETET in my journals, which stands for **E**ntry, **T**arget, **E**xit, and **T**ime frame (projected exit time). ETET are important parts of the trade. From this few elements, you can calculate your Payoff Ratio. It is also important to write down what happened to the trades. Did you hit your target price or are you stop out?

I will share with you some examples of how to fine-tune your strategy with your recorded trades in a trading journal:

- **If every trade loses money right from entry**. Relook your trading strategy.
- **If the trade was correct but did not hit the target price and was eventually stop out when it hit the cut loss price**. Adjust your target price, which may have been too high.
- **If the trade hit the stop-loss price first, causing you to exit the trade prematurely and later hit your target price**. Adjust your stop-loss price as it may have been too tight.

When you do adjustments to your trades, you will eventually become better and better. The problem is most people do not even record what or how they trade. Without the inputs, you cannot improve, as you do not know what went wrong. Now do you understand the importance of having a trading journal?

At this point, I also want to emphasise the importance of getting a good mentor. Sometimes, we become so involved in the trading that we cannot see ourselves. So it is important for someone to be there to guide you along. You have my contact at the end of the book. Feel free to add me on Facebook or we could meet at one of my seminars.

In the following pages, you can see some examples in Figures 8-3 and 8-4 to have a better idea as to how I record my trading journals.

Date	Stock	Entry	Target	Exit	Time	Setup	Source	Remarks
1/10/2013	Noble	0.935	0.97	0.9	5 days	Swing	ChartNexus	

Figure 8-3: Sample of trading journal

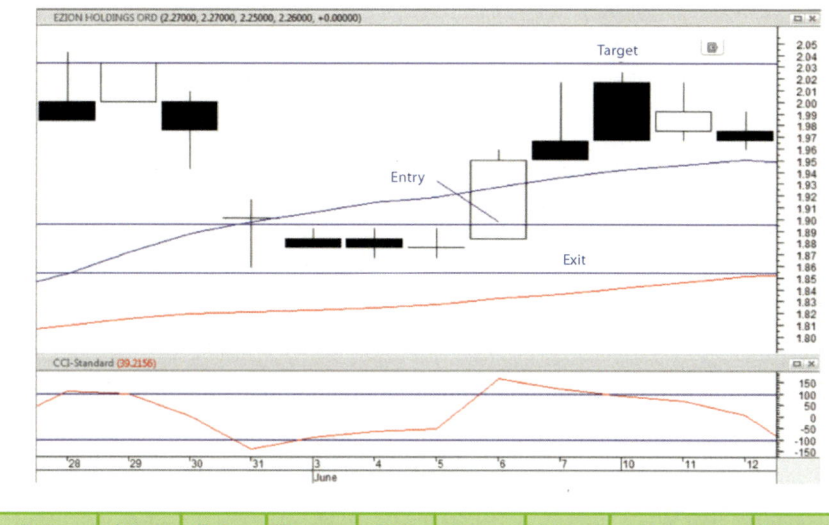

Date	Stock	Entry	Target	Exit	Time	Setup	Source	Remarks
6/6/2013	Ezion	1.895	2.03	1.855	5 days	Swing	ChartNexus	

Figure 8-4: Sample of trading journal

"The fruits of your trading or investment success will be in direct ratio to the honesty and sincerity of your own effort in keeping your own records, doing your own thinking, and reaching your own conclusions. You cannot wisely read a book on 'how to keep fit' and leave the physical exercise to another."
– Jesse Livermore

ETE determines the **Payoff Ratio** as well as the **Probability of Win**.

$$Payoff\ Ratio = \frac{(Target\ Price-Entry\ Price)}{(Entry\ Price-Exit\ Price)}$$

To be profitable in trading, we should seek a strategy with a **Payoff Ratio greater than 1**. That means the amount of potential profit made will generally be more than what you would potentially lose if the trade went sour. Say, for example, in every trade made, I will potentially either profit $100 or lose $60. Some trading strategies have a payoff ratio of less than 1, but are compensated with a high Probability of Win. This, to me, is rather risky and I would usually avoid such strategies. Many traders, especially new traders who adopt such strategies, could suffer big losses due to one bad trade, wiping out all their earlier small winnings! Do not be attracted to such quick small gains! Beware of this trap and, as much as possible, avoid strategies with payoff ratios of less than 1.

Probability of Win simply measures the number of wins versus the number of losses in a series of trades. Note the key word here is *series*. The ideal condition is to have a strategy with Probability of Win equal to 1. This means, you will have 100 wins out of 100 trades. This is wonderful, but in this realistic world, practically impossible! Not even for the best trader on Earth.

As much as possible, we look for a strategy where the **Probability of Win is at least 0.5**. That means that for every trade you made, the chances of winning will be 50%. Let us take coin tossing as an example. Each time you toss a coin, you will have 50% chance of getting heads and 50% chance of getting tails. Thus, if you toss the same coin 100 times, you are likely to get tails or heads half the time. What is the Probability of Win for the particular strategy you are using? You have to perform extensive back-testing to find out the answer. There are no shortcuts in trading. Do your homework!

Of course, we will try to look for strategies that give a higher Probability of Win. Nevertheless, be mindful and do not get trapped into looking for a strategy with 100% Probability of Win—which many amateur traders do. Instead of searching high and low for such a strategy, I strongly recommend you to use the effort writing trading journals, learning more about yourself. Remember Sun Tzu's teachings? Trust me that you will be far better off this way, compared to those who are still "wasting" time searching for the "perfect strategy". They will be very disappointed and eventually give up trading. I have seen too many such incidences!

Importance of Trading Psychology and Money Management

As traders, we are constantly looking for an edge over the market. This is like a casino having an edge over the players/punters by setting house rules that are in favour of the house. Nevertheless as traders, our edge against the market is small regardless of whether you are a super trader or a retail trader. That is why having a correct trading psychology coupled with good money management is so important in order to be a **sustainable** and **profitable** trader.

Under normal conditions, many can trade according to their own sets of trading and money management rules. But nothing can stop them from getting overconfident or greedy, which results in overtrading. Overtrading, in this case, means having a position too big for your portfolio. When a trade turns against them, they tend to lose "clarity" of thought and make emotional decisions.

For example, let's say under normal situations, cutting loss with a $500 loss may seem reasonable to them. They are able to cut loss according to their rules if the trade turns against them. But if they overtrade and are in a loss of $5,000 or more, cutting loss will be a painful decision! Not willing to lose that big sum of money, they will most likely hold, hoping and praying for the trade to return to their favour. This is not forgetting humans like to be right and cutting loss, to amateur traders, equates to being wrong! This "hoping" will continue until the amount is so big that it jeopardises their trading account.

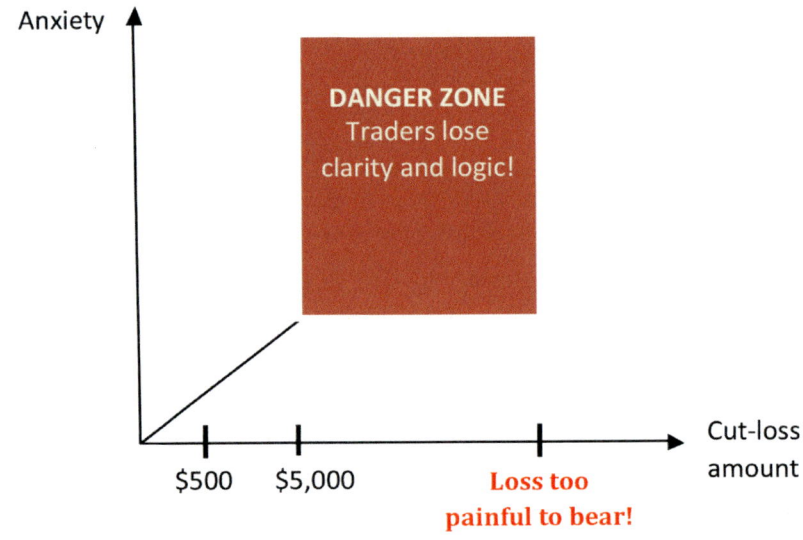

Figure 8-5: Graph illustrating Traders' Logic

From Figure 8-5, we can observe that the anxiety level for most traders skyrockets in the danger zone. This is just like why most people are unable to think logically or even panic when under stressful conditions. Under such trading situations, they will not think logically. More often than not, they try their luck "fighting" or betting against the market. We must avoid this zone as much as possible if your goal is to be a successful and profitable trader. This is also one of the key reasons why many traders, including seasoned ones, can make money along the way and suddenly lose all of it in one single trade due to overtrading. They may be skilful, but incorrect values as well as trading psychology can harm them and their trading career. I am sure you definitely do not want to enter this danger zone!

Have you heard of the quote "an angry mind is a narrow mind"? If you are angry, frustrated or anxious, you cannot think properly and execute according to plan. Most of the time, you will regret what you did after cooling down. The same applies to trading, when money is at stake. This is even worse when you believe that you are the owner of the money! Do you now see the importance of viewing yourself as a steward?

How many times have you heard that you need to stay calm when an unexpected emergency situation arises? Why is this so? This is because in a state of anxiety or panic, we are not able to react or behave in the way we would when in a calm state. Any decisions made in such a panicky state of mind will most likely be absurd and even unsound.

For trading, it is important to have comprehensive plans for exiting the market and make sure you follow closely to these trading strategy and rules. Always ensure you are not in the danger zone and avoid situations that expose you to it. You now know exactly what to do in order to stay away, right?

The Precession Effect

The Precession Effect can be defined simply thus: for every action taken, there will be a side effect arising at 90-degrees to the line of action. Figures 8-6 and 8-7 will give a clearer picture.

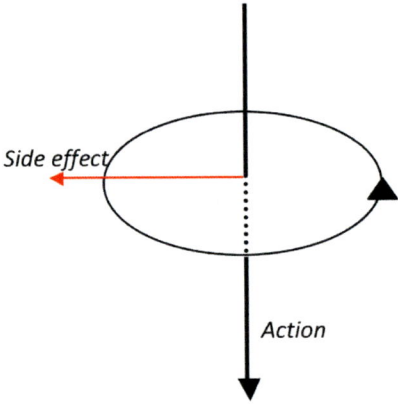

Figure 8-6: The Precession Effect

I always like to share this bee story with traders, or rather, the traders still struggling to be profitable. The main focus of the bees is to look for flowers so as to extract the nectar for honey. To the bees, extracting nectar is their main goal and purpose in life. The precession effect of such action by the bees is the pollination of flowers, which has a bigger impact on the bees' life. They may not be aware of that. But do you not agree that the bees will not have future generations if they do not pollinate the flowers today? Do you know that one third of the food we eat is from such pollination of flowers? To the bees, however, they are only concerned with extracting the nectar from the flowers, which is undeniably their main focus.

Figure 8-7: The bee story – true purpose of pollination

Exactly the same should be applied to trading. Most amateur traders usually focus on how much money to make, or that they want to make. They constantly look for a 100% sure-win strategy to make big profits and never to lose any. They strive to make a certain amount of money in a day to become millionaires in a short period of time. By setting such targets, this means traders are not prepared or willing to lose any money. With such thoughts and intentions, they are simply setting themselves up for failure in the long run. Well, it need not be too long, if you know what I mean.

Traders should focus on trading well instead, not how much money to make per trade, per day, or per month. What I mean by trading well is to follow your trading and money management rules religiously. Write in your trading journal every time a trade is made. When you trade well, money will be the tangible result resulting from the precession effect (Figure 8-8).

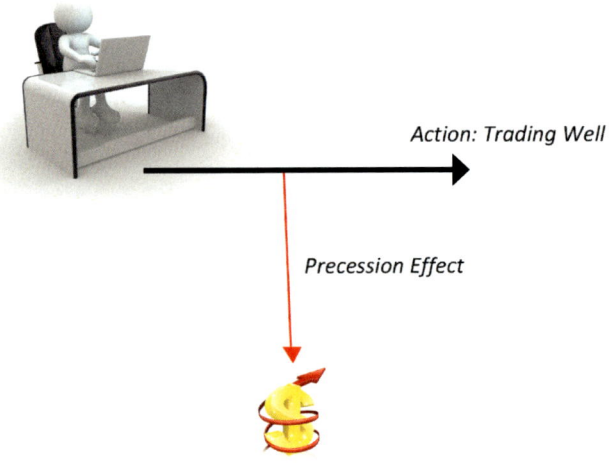

Figure 8-8: Trading well with the precession effect

If traders focus too much on money, they will likely ignore the importance of setting stop-loss, adopt poor position sizing techniques, get emotionally involved, and all other trading related problems will start streaming in like a tsunami. Remember and understand what your main focus in trading is.

On the other hand, I know exactly why many traders cannot focus on trading well when their purpose is solely on the money. For this, I have to tie it to Neuro-Linguistic Programming (NLP). Humans always want to be right and to do the "right" thing. In trading too, we tend to want to do the "right" thing, which is to take profit as this action makes us feel good. This turns into the common problem of traders taking profit prematurely. Such action inevitably affects the payoff ratio and your trading performance in the long run.

Taking a loss is admitting that they are wrong and humans do not like to be wrong. Thus, they avoid being wrong by not exiting the position and locking in the loss. Paper loss is not considered a loss to them, yet! This is the reason why many traders fall into the "danger zone" and eventually, only cut loss when the amount becomes too much to bear. Please take it from me that in trading, you will surely have losing trades. The number of times the trade goes wrong versus right depends on your strategy's Probability of Win. Putting the Precession Effect into perspective, as long as your strategy has a decent Probability of Win, you simply need to concentrate on trading well, follow your rules, and nothing else.

Setting Your Goals

As a trader, it is important for you to recognise and differentiate *Process Goals* and *Result Goals*.

In life, we often set result goals as society has taught us: results-oriented. Getting first in class or earning $100,000 a year are some examples of result goals we set for ourselves. Unfortunately, result goals are things we do not have complete control over. In trading, we cannot set result goals because we do not and cannot control the market. If you think you can, please seriously reconsider. You can know the market by studying the fundamentals or following the news closely. But you can never control the market. Even if the setup is perfect and most elements are in your favour, you can still lose money in the trade. As such, results are something no trader can control. Nevertheless, we can control the processes and our own behaviours. Therefore, traders should be setting **process goals** instead of result goals.

Process goals could be doing 30 successful ETET trades (according to predefined trading rules) in a month with good journaling. Points are scored when a correct ETET trade is executed according to the rules. Doing ETET trades is something you can have 100% control while the outcome of trades is something you cannot control. Do not be too bothered or upset with something you cannot control.

Many traders often get upset after a few losing trades and stop trading, blame the market, or search for another sure-win trading strategy. If you focus too much on result goals, you will start thinking that it is the strategy that is no good, causing you to lose money. You may also believe that trading is just not suitable for you and such thoughts may weaken your decision making process. All these will go into a negative spiral effect, taking you further from your goal of becoming a successful trader.

Stewardship or Ownership Mentality

Remember I mentioned stewardship and ownership in Chapter Two? Stewardship or ownership is a way of thinking that affects your psychology of trading. I strongly encourage you to set aside time and give some thought to it after reading this section. Take this seriously and you may gain a new positive perspective to trading.

If you think you are the "owner" of a new car, you will be careful with it. Even a small scratch may upset you. You will also spend much time maintaining and polishing the car to ensure it looks better than your neighbour's. Under such a situation, the car owns you and you become its "slave". On the other hand, if you are not the owner but the "steward" of the car, you will always think of ways to help others with it. You will be more concerned with how good you are as a steward of the car. You will be concerned with getting from one point to the other safely and effectively. Do you not think that the same goes for trading as well as for life?

With an ownership mentality, you tend to be emotional and cannot think and execute a trade properly according to your rules. This is especially when your money is involved. This is also the reason why fund managers tend to do better compared to retail traders. Fund managers are stewards of the money and their primary concern is to follow the rules so as to keep their job. As long as the fund managers trade according to the rules, they may not lose their job even if they lost money trading. To the fund managers, they are neither the boss nor owner of the money; they are simply temporary owners. With this thought, they are emotionally detached from the money, which makes them better traders.

Now you know why fund managers generally trade better? Do you want to be able to trade like a fund manager? Now you know exactly what to change in order to trade like them? How about fusing this with the Precession Effect?

Human Nature

Humans are naturally risk averse. We are afraid to lose what we have. This is one of the key reasons most traders find it difficult to cut loss or allow profits to run.

Let me draw a scenario to further illustrate this point. You have two boxes in front of you, which are Box A and Box B.

- In Box A: Three blue balls and one red ball
- In Box B: One red ball

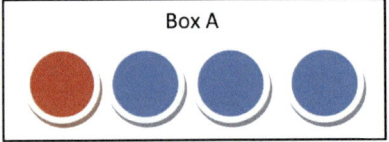 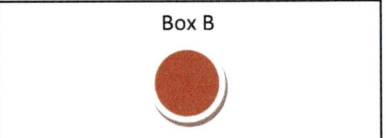

Note that you are not able to see inside the box and you do not know what you will be picking.

Game 1

In Box A, if you pick the red ball, you will gain $1,000. You will make $0 if you pick a blue ball.

In Box B, there is only one red ball, which you will gain $200.

With these conditions and having one chance to pick a ball from either box, which box will you put your hand into? Make your choice now before proceeding to the next game.

Game 2

In Box A, if you pick the red ball, you will lose $1,000. You will lose $0 if you pick a blue ball.

In Box B, there is only one red ball which you will lose $200.

Now, which box will you put your hand in?

I bet most will choose Box B in Game 1 as you will definitely make money. This is exactly the same thinking of many losing traders! Why they lose money in the long run is because they prefer taking profits prematurely.

In Game 2, did you pick Box A? I believe many of you were thinking that you would not be so unlucky as to pick that one red ball, right? I have another question for you: why are you exposing yourself to a chance of an outsized loss? This illustrates struggling traders who are reluctant to cut loss when in a losing trade, eventually only exiting the position when the loss is too big to bear (remembering the "danger zone").

To be successful in trading, you should be cutting your losses short while giving your profit a chance to run. It is just simply that! No other tricks or secret formula. This is a part of successful trading which goes against normal human logic.

Game 3

In Box A: Three blue balls and one red ball
- Blue ball – win $200
- Red Ball – lose $1,000

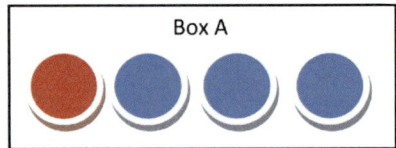

You have 100 chances to pick a ball from Box A. The ball that you picked will be put into the same box before picking the next ball again.

With probability as well as payoff ratio in mind, three out of every four balls you pick is blue, which makes you $600 richer. However, one out of every four balls you pick is red, which will wipe out all your winnings and put you $400 in debt.

This is just like what most traders do. They want to take profit when there is some money to take. Lady Luck may be smiling at them and they may enjoy a few consecutive wins, making them some money. More often than not, one bad trade is enough to wipe out all their winnings and put them in debt. Believe it or not, I have seen too many examples like that!

Do not forget one important truth: "No matter how great your strategy is, there will still be losing trades!"

Hopefully, this chapter makes you aware why you are still not a profitable trader yet. You are not able to change something you do not know or are unaware of. Therefore, with this awareness, I sincerely hope you are able to make the necessary positive changes *immediately*!

WHEN IT COMES TO MAKING MONEY, BE A RISK TAKER

WHEN IT COMES TO LOSING MONEY, BE RISK AVERSE

ALWAYS RIDE YOUR WINNERS AND CUT YOUR LOSSES QUICK

Learning Points

- The biggest problem is most new traders do not think and work hard enough.

- When you are trading, you are betting your judgement against someone else's.

- There is an outer war and an inner war in trading; you need to win both wars in order to be a successful trader.

- Trading without a journal is like stepping on the car accelerator with your eyes closed.

- To ensure success in trading, you need to have a feedback loop for your actions.

- It is possible to lose money on a right trade and win money on a wrong trade. The key is to identify which is the action of a successful trader.

- To be a successful trader, focus on trading well instead of how much money you can make.

- When buying, ask yourself, "Is there any reason why I should not buy?" If you cannot find any reason, that will be the right trade. When buying, do not ask yourself if there is a reason you should buy, because you can always find one.

- Good traders ask themselves where their stop-loss is and the risk associated with each and every trade.

- Bad traders ask themselves what price they should sell at, because they are sure that the trade will move in their favour.

- Know your plans before opening a new position.

- Only set process goals because result goals are out of your control.

- In order to think like a fund manager, you must adopt a stewardship mentality.

- Cut your losers, ride your gainers without fear of losing what you won.

- Be slow to take profits and be quick to cut losses.

- When it comes to making money, people are risk averse; when it comes to losing money, people are risk takers.

Exercise

- Importance of having a feedback loop.

    a. Trader A will verbally describe the drawing below in Figure 8-9 to Trader B. Trader B has to produce the drawing accordingly, without asking any questions.

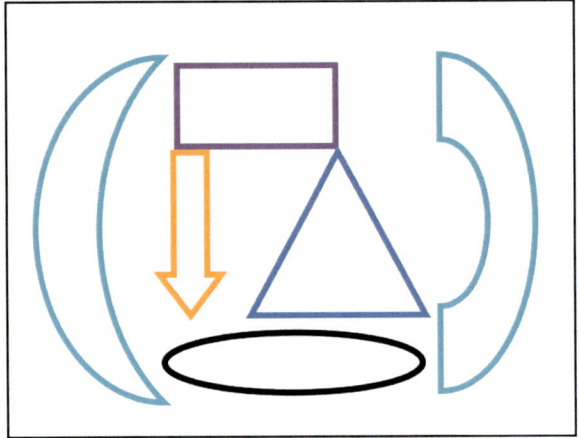

Figure 8-9: Worksheet – no feedback loop

    b. Now, Trader A will describe verbally the next drawing in Figure 8-10 to Trader B. Trader B has to reproduce the drawing and is allowed to ask as many questions as he/she wants. Trader A will answer the questions.

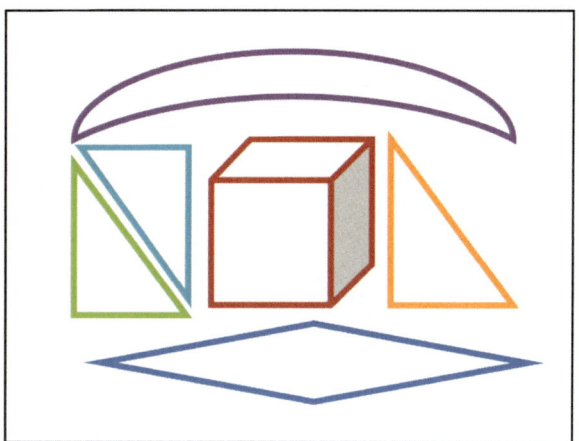

Figure 8-10: Worksheet – with feedback loop

Compare the two drawings produced by Trader B with the originals. I believe the second one, where Trader B can ask questions, would be more similar to the original drawing? Do you now understand the importance of having a feedback loop? Can you relate that to writing a trading journal?

- Are you writing in your trading journal? How are you going to write it?

_____

_____

_____

_____

- Under what circumstances in life are you a steward and/or owner? How can you be a steward in life as well as trading?

- What are your process goals in trading?

- Looking at the Trader's Logic Graph (Figure 8-5 on page 148), where is your cut-loss amount before entering the danger zone?

- What are your perspectives in trading before and after reading this chapter? How and what will you do to be a better trader?

9 PERSONALITY AND PEOPLE

Follower: If I follow all the laws of enlightenment, how long before I can gain enlightenment?

Buddha: One year...

Follower: What if I work harder?

Buddha: Three years.

Follower: But what if I work even harder to gain enlightenment?

Buddha: Five years!

S ad to say, the same principle applies in trading. If you focus only on making money, you will take an even longer time to achieve your trading goals. You will drift further and further away from your objective of trading well. The more you focus on money, the less you will be able to trade well. As a result, the more you are unable to make money and gain wealth from trading.

Different traders behave differently due to their own unique personalities. Different strategies are suited for different folks. Thus, it is important to first understand yourself.

Personality Test

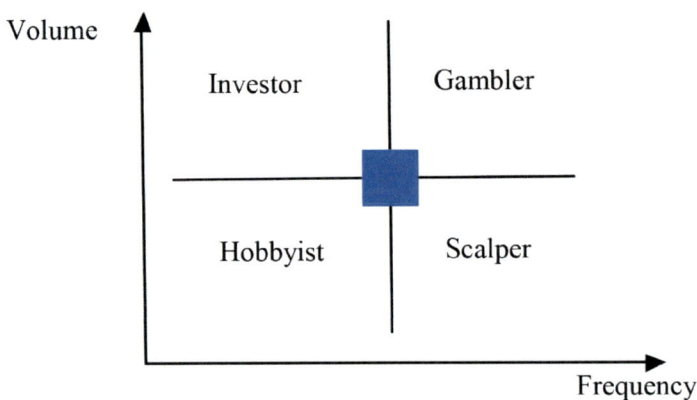

Figure 9-1: The trader personality

Through my experiences and studies made over these years, I have formulated a personality test that you can use to better identify yourself. On the vertical axis (Figure 9-1), "volume" depicts the amount of money risked on every trade made while the horizontal axis "frequency" indicates how often a trade is made.

It is important to identify which quadrant you belong to as it indicates your personality. I cannot stress any further the importance of knowing yourself while knowing the market. I do understand that most of the time, we need to get involved in the market, or in looking for the "best" strategy, before you can correctly identify which quadrant you belong to. Some take six months, some one year, and others several years, depending on your goals and how committed you are. Some traders may, over time, evolve from one quadrant to another, or lead in more than one quadrant. No matter what, **it is extremely important to identify which quadrant you belong to as it states what kind of trader you are, and this determines the necessary actions or plans for you to take in order to stay profitable.**

Investor

Traders in the "Investor" quadrant usually trade large volumes but less frequently. One good example is Warren Buffet. He does many studies on a company before deciding to buy the stocks. When he buys, more likely than not, it is in huge volumes.

Traders in this quadrant are more likely to be analytical. They study the inside out of the market they are in, as well as the stocks of the companies before making a decision. Once it is made, they stick to their plans and execute accordingly without fail.

Being analytical also means that traders in this quadrant do not make hasty decisions. Every decision is backed by solid research. Although in the market you may wish to be a little more careful, such action can be a double-edged sword. It means that traders may likely be buried too much into research to seek a definite answer that they miss good entry opportunities. As such, it is important that traders in the "Investor" quadrant know exactly where their strengths and weaknesses are, in order to be a more competent trader. They can have a simple checklist to qualify a trading decision. Once all criteria are satisfied, simply execute the trade as planned, forgoing the urge to do further studies or information gathering. Quit searching for addition information or confirmations, which may result in losing a trading opportunity that satisfies your trading strategy and rules. An alternative is to give someone you trust the checklist, have him or her execute the trade for you once all entry criteria are met.

Those in the "Investor" quadrant usually adopt strategies for position trading. They leverage on big move in price, hence tapping on the momentum of current trend. They have to be patient to see the results. Remember I mentioned earlier that position trading accumulates wealth while swing trader earns income? Investors may wish to hone their skills, building capabilities to do both long and short-term trading. More importantly, find out exactly what do you want to achieve in trading and do your due diligence to work towards it!

DO NOT ANALYSE TILL YOU ARE PARALYSED

Gambler

Traders in the "Gambler" quadrant behave very differently from those in the "Investor". They trade in high volumes very frequently. They are able to make decisions promptly and execute trades without much consideration or fear.

Traders in this quadrant are usually able to overcome losses easily while trying to make back what they lose with one big winning trade. They may or may not have a strategy to follow. Even if they do, entry and exit decisions made may not adhere to the rules.

Traders in the "Gambler" quadrant need to understand their purpose of trading. What do they want to achieve from it? Is it excitement or is it a sense of satisfaction? Is the market a gambling den in which to strike a jackpot? If you are serious in being successful as a trader in the long run, you should try staying away from the "Gambler" quadrant. Always have a plan when executing a trade. Trade according to what you planned. Do practise paper trading using your trial account to ensure you are able to execute according to your trading plan. Once that is established, try trading a live account with 20% of your trading account. Slowly grow the amount involved as you start to see results.

I strongly encourage traders in this quadrant to seriously work on their behaviour so as to shift to another quadrant. That is, if you are determined to be a profitable trader. Stop trading until you have managed to work on yourself.

Try reading books covering trading psychology. Some of the good reads are *Mind over Market* by Denise Shull, *Daily Trading Coach* by Brett Steenbarger, and *Trading in the Zone* by Mark Douglas.

The other alternative is to fully automate your trades. That would mean designing a system that you believe in, leaving entries and exits to the computer (based on the criteria of the strategy). Doing so greatly minimises emotions. All you have to do is to constantly back-test your system, ensuring it is up to date according to current market situations. Be sure to adopt proper money management in all the trades you make. Do not overtrade!

UNDERSTAND THE PURPOSE OF WHY YOU TRADE

Scalper

Traders in the "Scalper" quadrant are those who go in and out of markets very frequently in small amounts. Such traders have a trading plan in mind and execute their plan with exact accuracy without room for error. They want to be right 100% of the time. Failure is not an option for them.

The need to be always right can be a setback for traders in this quadrant. Once they encounter a few losing trades, they may feel lousy or helpless. They can get so disturbed that they lose concentration for the whole day. Some may even give up trading ultimately, thinking that it is not their cup of tea. Every trader should know that there is no fool-proof strategy or Holy Grail in trading. Do not give up the strategy if you encounter one or a few losing streaks, which is perfectly normal in trading. As explained in earlier chapters, we do not know the sequence of winning or losing trades. What we can know is the Probability of Win over a series of trades. As long as it is more than 0.5, with a Payoff Ratio of more than 1, you will definitely be a profitable trader in the long run.

Do not fall into the common trap of finding a sure-win strategy as that will keep you going in circles. You will never ever achieve your trading goals this way. Do not get too obsessed in being 100% right. It is alright to be wrong sometimes, especially in trading where the market is so dynamic.

Nobody can be absolutely right all the time—do you not agree that this is the fact of life? You should not beat yourself up as long as the decisions you made there and then were logical, adhering to your principles and values. What is more important than always trying to make a correct decision is to learn from experience. It is only through experience that we gain our wisdom. As such, do not be too hard on yourself when your trades do not quite go the way you think it should be. Let it go. Look out for the next entry opportunity, in accordance to your strategy and rules. Instead of insisting to achieve 100% wins for all your trades, consider shifting this unrealistic requirement to following your trading strategy and rules at all times. If you are able to do this, you are on your path to being a profitable trader!

BE BRAVE ENOUGH TO ACCEPT DEFEAT

Hobbyist

Last but not least, traders in the "Hobbyist" quadrant tend to be inconsistent in trading. They trade frequently in small amounts, which could appear as if they are simply trying their luck. As such, they are not being too serious in trading. Traders in the "Hobbyist" quadrant tend to hop from strategy to strategy, looking for "Holy Grails". As their losses are usually small, they are not too concerned with applying proper money management.

If you happen to fall in this quadrant, it is time for you to rethink what trading is to you. Do you just want to have a feel of it? Do you simply wish to have the thrill of putting money into the market and hope for the best? Or do you wish to trade because you heard many success stories and did not want to miss the boat? No matter what the reason is, do ensure that the amount involved is manageable so as to avoid big losses.

Could it be that you do not have the time to constantly monitor the market? If this is the reason, you may wish to reconsider the time frame you are trading in. Consider trading in a longer time frame, for example, 4-hourly chart, daily or even weekly charts. If not, you can also consider automating your strategy, so that the programme can execute trades on its own based on your requirements. Minimum supervision is required from you this way.

FORMULATE A GOAL AND EXECUTE THE ACTION PLAN

Which quadrant do you belong to?

Investors
- Prefer to work with checklists
- Love reading research reports
- Analytical in nature
- Follow the mind rather than the heart
- Able to stay calm under intense or stress situations
- Do not like volatility or randomness
- Focus on the business rather than price
- Hope to buy more at lower price when price falls

Gamblers
- Enjoys thrills
- Love tips
- Follow heart rather than mind
- Do not like to follow rules
- Enjoys the thrill of gambling
- Look at the market regularly
- Focus on the profits
- Like volatility and randomness
- Attend seminars regularly and buy all stocks recommended
- Will keep buying/selling while waiting for price to reserve in my favour

Hobbyists
- Adventurous in trying out new things
- Follow heart rather than mind
- Love tips
- Short attention span
- Focus on not losing
- Follow the gurus' recommendation or the crowd
- Attend seminars regularly but don't take action
- Ignore or do nothing when trade move against me

Scalpers
- Want to see returns fast
- Love to watch the time and sales
- Follow the mind only
- Perfectionists
- Able to make quick decisions
- Able to stay focused for an extended period of time
- Focus on risk
- Like volatility
- Cut loss immediately when prices drop

Figure 9-2: The Trader Quadrants

There are many personality tests available (as well as many online) that you can take to determine the kind of trader you are. I encourage you to do some of the tests to better understand yourself. A good test is by world-renowned investment expert Dr Van K. Tharp: www.tharptradertest.com/default.aspx

People

We always talk about strategies and knowledge, but not much attention is put into the community you hang out with. The community you are with will influence the way you trade. If, for example, you are with a community that trades well (regularly discussing stop-loss, Probability of Win, Risk/Reward Ratio, etc.), your chances of success becomes higher. In contrast, if you are with a group of pundits who just wish to make bets, who have no idea what cutting loss is, the likelihood of you gaining success in trading is extremely low. In this community, you will most likely act and trade like them, simply looking for quick bucks without wanting to put in much effort to attain sustainable success.

One of my goals is to create a community of like-minded people speaking the same language. Things such as trade setups, stop-loss, target price, and position sizing are some of the things professional traders talk about. Once this community is formed, a positive upward spiral will be created, benefitting members of the community. Most traders who fail often want to find a quick fix, take short-cuts, and hence, regress. I believe one of the reasons why most traders do not form communities is because they resist change. They find it a hassle. Understand the need for a community. If you want to be a successful trader, you have to be diligent. Work for it!

Every Tuesday, I have clients gathering to talk about the same thing. Remember that my purpose is to form a community of like-minded people speaking the same language. With this, I form groups of about eight traders per group to:

- **Set Common Goals that every team member works toward**. They encourage and remind one another to trade well.
- **Set Context, to form ground rules agreed by every member**. For example, make it compulsory to meet every Tuesday, present a stock every week, or share a successful trade.
- **Promote good Communication between team members**. Repeat what is good or right in trading. This ensures that the trading rules stick in the members' mind. Traders can do so face to face or via social media. Regular meetings for communication is preferred.

This is what I call the "3C"s of community. The community you are in should preferably have trading styles similar to yours and trade similar instruments as well. This will ensure that everyone can better understand one another during discussions.

Power of Community

If you leave a burning coal alone, it will cool down and die out very quickly. But if you burn chunks of coal together, they will burn stronger and longer. We tend to regress over time when there is no accountability. Therefore, when there is a feedback system where everybody is helping everybody, you will tend to do better. You can also call it peer pressure, which, in this case, is a good influence for you to continuously improve. Not only does it improve your technical competency, it also helps in the emotional side of trading. Set ground rules so that everyone is contributing and enriching this pool of knowledge.

IN THE COMMUNITY, EVERYONE MUST SHARE AND CONTRIBUTE

Conclusion

I hope you are able to understand more about yourself after reading this chapter. I stress again the importance of knowing yourself and the markets as well as the products you are trading, in order to be profitable in this business. Take some time to answer the questionnaires, which I believe will be beneficial to you.

Once you know more about yourself, your trading style, the markets and products you are trading, find a community to hang out with. Nevertheless, do be aware of the quality of the people within the community. Ensure they are an asset to you. You, too, must contribute to the community. This is one sure way to improve your trading results. If possible, look for a community with a majority of members in the "Investor" and "Scalper" quadrants.

Learning Points

- Knowing yourself is as important, if not more so than knowing the market.

- Are you an investor, scalper, gambler or hobbyist?

- You can change yourself, by changing the environment and people around you.

- Set common goals that are aligned with every team member.

- Set common context or rules so that all know how to succeed.

- Communication on context and goals ensures that everyone is on the right path.

Exercise

• Which quadrant do you belong to?

_____

_____

• Now that you know what kind of trader you are, what is your action plan to become a consistent profitable trader?

a. What are your trading process goals?

_____

b. Which products will you use?

_____

c. What time frame will you trade (Intra-day, Swing or Position)?

_____

d. How well do you understand your strategy?

_____

e. What is your position sizing plan?

_____

f. Which quadrants do you belong to?

_____

g. Have you identified a community to participate?

_____

EPILOGUE

I don't believe it. It is finally over. I must say writing this book has been painful for me. It took much longer than expected and I constantly wanted to "improve" on it such that it was almost impossible to settle on the final version. On the other hand, given the chance, I would still do this again. My intention is to share with others my trading journey and what I have learnt, and I am glad to have written this book.

Writing a book is almost the same as trading. The journey is not going to be smooth but it will be worth it. I hope that with this book, you will continue to learn and trade well. There is no replacement for hard work. I am still learning new things about the market and myself.

Here are some parting thoughts.

Teach. The best and fastest way to learn is to teach. Unless you understand the subject matter thoroughly, you are not able to answer every question.

Give. When you give, you are telling yourself that you have enough. This is important for your psychological well-being. The Bible mentions giving 10% of what you have. I think more importantly, what it suggests is the attitude of giving. Give with a cheerful heart and give anonymously.

Live. Trading and making money is a means to an end. Enjoy time with the ones you love. I do not think any trader will ever regret not taking a particular trade to his or her deathbed. Instead, the most probable regret, like many other individuals', is not spending enough time with your loved ones.

If you are committed to being successful in trading, you are welcome to join my community to help yourself to become a better trader. I started growing a community so that we can share our resources with one another. This is also the place where I will share some of my latest thoughts on the market.

- **Facebook**
  www.facebook.com/groups/mastermindtrader
  www.facebook.com/collinseowfanpage

- **Twitter**
  www.twitter.com/collinseow

- **Blog**
  www.collinseow.com

I have created a series of follow-ups for this book. You can attend the seminars conducted by me. I hope to see you at one of them, and I would be happy to autograph your book. Finally, let's keep in touch through my Facebook and Twitter. Keep learning and never give up doing good.

RESOURCES

I n this bonus section, I share with you the resources I frequently use that might be useful to you too. It is a fine line between too little research and too much. Nobody can tell you how much is enough— only you know the answer. Thus, it is important for every trader to know his or herself and the market to be successful in trading.

As traders, we must be aware of the economic situation so as to have a general idea of how the market is performing. This is so even if you are purely a chart technician. Yet, too much research will also leave us confused and unable to make quick and sound decisions. So, how much is enough?

To be honest, I do not have single specific answers to these. It all depends on your trading goals, personality, and how much time you can or are willing to spend on trading. No matter what, you must always obey and follow your trading rules, and couple this with good money management. **Disregarding this is a sure way to fail in trading**!

Not only will I share the resources I frequently use myself, I will also reveal to you a few simple yet powerful exit strategies. You are welcome to download these in a special section at my website at www.

thesystematictraderbook.com/gifts. A good strategy requires clear and definite entry and exit criteria. You may enter a trade under perfect conditions, but a poor exit will still cost you money. It is important that you have an exit strategy planned even before entering a trade.

> **BELIEVE YOU SHOULD UNDERSTAND BY NOW THAT IN TRADING, YOU PLAN YOUR TRADES AND TRADE YOUR PLANS.**

Key Resources

Bloomberg
Bloomberg is one of the leaders in global business and financial information, enabling customers to make smarter, faster, more informed business decisions.

Website: www.bloomberg.com

FreeStockCharts
This is the site where the charts are free, the data is streaming in real-time and the features beat expensive trading platforms. FreeStockCharts. com has one goal, which is to make you a successful investor in the stock market. Be prepared for many "ah ha!" moments as you begin this exciting journey.

Website: www.freestockcharts.com

Google Finance

Get updated financial news, company portfolios with stock screeners available all in one place. You can even customise your dashboard.

Website: www.google.com/finance

I3investor

The I3investor portal provides a platform for traders and investors to discuss and collaborate with other investors online. The I3investor community generates over 50,000 comments and posts each month. One key feature of this site is the "Price Target", which shares with readers the target price of a selected stock or company.

Website: www.i3investor.com

Investopedia

Investopedia is the largest website devoted entirely to education. Investopedia was started in June 1999 as an unbiased source to learn about investing. This is a very useful website you need to visit.

Website: www.investopedia.com

Investing.com

Founded in 2007, Investing.com is a definitive source for tools and information relating to the financial markets such as real-time quotes and streaming charts, up-to-date financial news, technical analysis, broker directory and listings, an economic calendar, and tools and calculators. The site provides in-depth information on Indices and Stocks, Commodities, Currencies, Futures and Options, and Rates & Bonds.

Website: www.investing.com

MarketWatch

MarketWatch, published by Dow Jones & Co., tracks the pulse of markets for engaged investors with more than 16 million visitors per month. The site is a leading innovator in business news, personal finance information, real-time commentary, and investment tools and data, with dedicated journalists generating hundreds of headlines, stories, videos and market briefs a day from 10 bureaus in the U.S., Europe, and Asia.

Website: www.marketwatch.com

Next Insight

Next Insight covers selected briefings organised by listed companies for analysts and fund managers. It does exclusive interviews with CEOs of selected companies, writes key content of clients' annual reports, including the financial and operations review, as well as producing content for publications such as CFA Singapore's newsletter. Not only does Next Insights provide and moderate a forum for readers to discuss stocks, it has a "Target Prices" tab which shares targeted price of selected stocks for readers' reference.

Website: www.nextinsight.net

POEMS

Phillip's Online Electronic Mart System, or more commonly known as POEMS, is the pioneer for Singapore's online share trading established by Phillip Securities Pte Ltd in 1996.

Website: www.poems.com.sg

share818.com

share818.com is the website owned by Alpha Alliance Technologies LLP. The website is a platform providing financial services related to stocks trading information and includes stock screening, stock charting, performance tracking, stock reviews, forums, and TA articles, etc.

Website: www.share818.com

Shares Investment (Singapore)

Published by Pioneers & Leaders (Publishers) since July 1995, Shares Investment (Singapore) has grown from strength to strength, garnering admirable reviews from the investing public and luminaries in the financial industry. Notably, Shares Investment (Singapore) enjoys the unwavering support from prominent local stock-broking houses, amongst many others UOB-Kay Hian, Phillip Securities, Kim Eng Securities, and DBS Vickers Securities—in all accounting for more than 30,000 readers.

Website: www.sharesinv.com

ShareInvestor Pte Ltd

ShareInvestor is a financial internet media and technology company that owns one of the largest investor relations networks in Asia. ShareInvestor provides market data tools and financial applications to institutional and retail investors.

Website: www.shareinvestor.com

Singapore Remisiers

Unlike other financial portals, this site has a forum that allows only remisiers to contribute their views and opinions of any nature relating to the financial industry, or try to answer questions about specific stocks and/or its derivatives. This, in turn, is open to the public for viewing only. As such, the niche is to create a platform where clients and the investing public can get an insight into what the dealing fraternity has to offer in addition to those of other business institutions like fund management firms, stock brokerages, exchanges, and banks. Under the "Research" tab, you can find many reports and research that can be useful for your studies.

Website: www.remisiers.org

Securities Investors Association (Singapore) or SIAS

SIAS is the largest organised investor lobby group in Asia, with almost 70,000 retail investors as members. It is run by a Management Committee comprising of professionals who are volunteers. It actively promotes Investor Education, Corporate Governance and Transparency and is the watchdog for investor rights in Singapore. To date, SIAS has successfully organised over 700 investor education programmes ranging from basic investment seminars for novices to certificate courses for investment savvy investors.

Website: www.sias.org.sg

Singapore Exchange
Singapore Exchange (SGX) is the Asian Gateway, connecting investors in search of Asian growth to corporate issuers in search of global capital. You can also check for latest market information and price of local stocks here.

Website: www.sgx.com

Thomas Reuters
Thomson Reuters is one of the world's leading sources of intelligent information for businesses and professionals.

Website: www.reuters.com

The Pattern Site
Thomas N. Bulkowski created ThePatternSite.com in November 2006 and the site had, by March 2009, received over 50,000 visits in one month. As of January 2011, it has grown to over 80,000. In 2010, the number of visits peaked at 932,172 for the year. ThePatternSite.com has

more than 650 pages of investment information, including a daily blog and software, all for free.

Website: www.thepatternsite.com

Technical Analysts Society Singapore

Technical Analysts Society Singapore (TASS) is a non-profit organisation which serves as a forum for traders and investors interested in using technical analysis methodologies for their trading and investment. TASS is affiliated society of IFTA, International Federation of Technical Analysts.

Website: www.tass.org.sg

Yahoo! Finance Singapore

At Yahoo! Singapore Finance, you can get free stock quotes, business news, portfolio management resources, a currency converter, international market data, and many other financial news.

Website: http://sg.finance.yahoo.com

FREE BONUSES

To thank you for purchasing this book, we would like to reward you with the following free bonuses:

Bonus #1

A bonus chapter entitled "5 secrets your remisier won't tell you about the stock market". If you are serious about winning BIG in the stock market, you won't want to wait another day to read this bonus chapter!

Bonus #2

A 4-hour Trading Bootcamp conducted in Singapore to help you get the most out of this book and start taking action.

Bonus #3

Gain access to training videos that will help you understand more about the stock market and how you can leverage the latest trading strategies to achieve consistent results.

CLAIM YOUR FREE BONUSES FROM

www.thesystematictraderbook.com/gifts

ABOUT THE AUTHOR

Collin Seow is a qualified Chartered Portfolio Manager (CPM) holding a Certified Financial Technician (CFTe) qualification, and a member of MENSA Singapore and Technical Analysts Society Singapore (TASS). He is also a trainer with CyberQuote (a member of PhillipCapital), and also the inventor of the stock trading softwares, TradersGPS and CSI Trading System.

Awarded the Top 10 Achievers in PhillipCFD for the last four consecutive years, Collin is also a regular speaker at conferences and seminars such as Shares Investment Conference, ShareInvestor INVEST Carnival, Phillip iFest, and MetaStock Conference.

He is a columnist for *Shares Investment* and *Tradeable*, and was featured as one of the traders in the national bestselling book, *Secrets of Highly Profitable Traders*. He also writes at his popular blog www.collinseow.com

Made in the USA
Middletown, DE
03 March 2019